Elements of Likability:
The New Science of Charm, Wit, Small Talk, and Social Intelligence

By Patrick King
Social Interaction and Conversation Coach at
www.PatrickKingConsulting.com

Table of Contents

CHAPTER 1: THE SECRET TO BEING CHARMING — 7

WHAT ON EARTH IS INVERSE CHARISMA? — 9
CHEMISTRY THROUGH PLAYFULNESS — 18
MASTERING CONVERSATIONAL RECEPTIVENESS — 25
QUIET LISTENING VS. LOUD LISTENING — 32

CHAPTER 2: OVERCOMING SHYNESS, NERVES AND INSECURITY — 41

THE 10-SECOND CONVERSATION TRICK — 42
SPEAK UP! — 47
THREE LEVELS OF CONVERSATION — 54
FROM SHALLOW TO DEEP — 63

CHAPTER 3: HOW TO SPEAK SO THAT PEOPLE CAN HEAR YOU — 73

THE MYSTERY OF THE JENNIFER ANISTON NEURON — 74
PEOPLE LOVE FAMILIAR STORIES — 81
ASKING FOLLOW-UP QUESTIONS — 88
THE CASE FOR SPOILERS — 95

CHAPTER 4: THE TOOLS OF THE TRADE   103

Long and short pauses   103
"Click" with someone through fast responses   109
The anatomy of a perfect compliment   115
Stay present, stay connected   125

CHAPTER 5: NAVIGATING CONFLICT, MISUNDERSTANDING, AND DISAGREEMENT   135

Language is everything   135
Magic words that smooth over conflict   144
Science-backed ways to end (or escape) a conversation   153

BONUS CHAPTER: CONVERSATION PROMPTS   163

Chapter 1: The secret to being charming

What makes a person likeable?

When people say someone is *charming*, what exactly are they talking about?

And what does it really mean to say you're a skilled communicator?

Though it may seem like the dark arts of the social butterfly are mysterious and hard to understand, the truth is that being a good conversationalist is something *anyone* can learn to do–even you!

However, most of the conventional advice out there is riddled with misconceptions about what it actually means to be a likeable, emotionally intelligent person capable of healthy communication. In fact, in this book, we're going to see that **many common assumptions about good conversation are exactly the opposite of what you'd expect.**

Connecting with others, building rapport, and finding that special "vibe" between two people… it's normal, it's human, and it's definitely accessible to you, no matter how much you may have struggled socially in the past. However, it's also true that to improve our conversation skills, we need to radically shift our mindset. We need to be ready and willing to learn how to approach other people in a way that may be completely new and unfamiliar.

In the chapters that follow, we'll explore in detail the attitude and approach most reliably associated with "charisma," as well as look at practical ways to overcome shyness and social awkwardness. We'll look at small tweaks that you can make to your everyday communication so that people really understand you. We'll also explore how you can more fully understand others, a skill that is just as important for effective communication. Finally, whenever you throw unpredictable human beings together, there will inevitably be friction and tensions. That's why we'll also be considering a few strategies to help you navigate your way through awkwardness and disagreement.

We'll look at the latest scientific research as well as expert opinions from research psychologists, linguists, couples' counsellors, FBI negotiators, and neuroscientists–all to ensure that we are gathering together sound wisdom about the art and science of communication. By the end of this book, my hope is that you feel more at ease in yourself and more genuinely curious about other people, and feel confident in how to reach out and connect with them.

All you'll need is the courage to try something new, and the willingness to have a little fun with it. First things first, though: we need to learn a skill that may well be the opposite of what you're expecting, namely, the art of inverse charisma.

What on earth is inverse charisma?

"I've learned that people will forget what you said, people will forget what you did, but people will never forget how you made them feel."

Maya Angelou

One of the biggest and most effective mindset shifts any of us can make when improving our conversation skills is this: **it's always far more effective to make other people feel valued than it is to get others to see our value.** This principle has been called *inverse charisma*, and it certainly does go against many of our automatic assumptions about charm and confidence.

Here's a fun thought experiment: try to remember the last time you had a truly enriching and enjoyable interaction with someone. Literally set this book aside for a moment and try to recall a recent conversation that left you feeling really, really good. Got it?

Now, bearing this specific conversation in mind, think carefully about exactly what it was that made the entire encounter so memorable.

After the conversation, did you think to yourself, "Wow! That person is so charming and charismatic! What an amazing and interesting person, and how captivating his stories were! I just loved how confident he was. And intelligent, too"?

Well, maybe you felt that way. I'm willing to bet, however, that what struck you was how good *you* felt to be in that person's presence. The vibe was great, there might have been some fun chemistry and energy, and rather than feeling like you were in the hallowed presence of someone else's charisma, *it was you yourself who felt somehow special.*

How many of us assume that in order to be charming and well-liked, we have to somehow puff ourselves up and make sure others really understand just how awesome we are? Maybe we spend a lot of effort finding ways to make ourselves look good, or we think we need to work hard to be funny, tell a good story, or have impressive things to share so that others think we're interesting, or sexy, or unique, or whatever. We might imagine that charismatic people are loud, gregarious, smooth, and somehow a little bit sparklier and more glamorous than everyone else. If we could only be a little more like them, we think, then we too would deserve to be found extra-likable.

But this is not a description of a likable person. If anything, it's a description of a celebrity. It's about ego. If your goal is to connect deeply and authentically with others, to have people understand you and like you, to craft enjoyable and generative conversations, and to build plenty of genuine relationships with people around you–then your best bet is not to cultivate charisma, but inverse charisma. **This requires dropping the ego, not elaborating on it.**

The irony is that when you can make others feel like they are captivating, interesting, valued, and well-regarded for their contribution and insight, you automatically make them like you more, and they'll want to spend time with you.

You don't have to be:

- An extrovert
- Beautiful or handsome
- Ultra-intelligent or well-educated
- Super unusual, unique, or creative
- A stand-up comedian
- Witty
- Attractive or alluring
- A "big" personality
- Confident

Cast your own mind back to the people you have most loved and cherished in your own life, or the conversations that were most fun and illuminating for you, and you will see that the other person likely had few, if any, of the above credentials! This is good news because it means you don't need them, either.

Shift the spotlight

Instead of seeing conversation as an arena in which you have to showcase your own personality, entertain others, or somehow prove your worth, take the pressure off. Understand that in a big way, it's not about you at all.

Shift the "spotlight" onto the other person and make them feel like the most captivating, interesting, and lovable person in the room.

If you're reading this book, chances are that not all parts of the social game come easily to you. However, inverse charisma not only brings you social success more quickly, but it also helps you create fun, genuine connections with way less stress and anxiety.

There is an anecdote about Winston Churchill's wife, Lady Clementine Churchill. She is said to have hosted a dinner party one day, to which two presidential candidates had been invited. After the dinner, she remarked that one candidate had seemed like the most interesting person in the world... whereas the other candidate had made her feel like *she* was the most interesting person in the world. You probably don't need to think about it too much to guess which man Lady

Churchill found most charming, charismatic, and likeable!

Here's a rather stable fact about human nature that many of us forget: **people don't really care how awesome you are**. They don't really care if you're accomplished, intelligent, beautiful, or rich. You may be able to inspire a little awe or jealousy by being superior in these ways, but the truth is that in other people's eyes, none of this alone makes you the least bit more likeable or enjoyable to spend time with.

Instead, people care about, well, themselves. People (you included) want to feel that others see, hear, and understand them. They want to feel accepted, liked, and listened to. They want to feel interesting and valuable.

Human beings enter into conversations because, on some level, they want to connect. Genuine human connection makes us feel like we belong, like others can see and hear us, and like there is a place for us in the world. We all yearn to know that when we speak and share ourselves, our contribution will be received warmly–maybe even joyfully.

When we shift the spotlight to addressing this deep human need instead of our own ego, we change our entire perspective and rethink the purpose of conversation in the first place.

A common way to see conversation is as a place where we have to: prove our worth, hustle for attention and approval, impress or entertain, convince or persuade, or somehow make the other person understand that we are right, worthy, desirable, or whatever the case may be. From this perspective, conversation devolves into a series of tips and tricks, pick-up lines, and a whole lot of self-absorption. Trying to be more charismatic by looking at conversation in this way is always doomed to fail because of one simple reason: it centers *you*.

An alternative way to view conversation is to see it as a place where we can: encounter another fascinating and totally unique individual, learn from them, enjoy them, and mutually create a fun, shared moment of connection. From this perspective, conversation becomes expansive and transformative, and far bigger than the egos of the individuals taking part. If we focus on the person we are communicating with and on the connection we are establishing, we will always succeed because we are no longer centering ourselves.

The great thing about this mindset shift is that, well, it's *fun*. When you think about it, self-absorption can be extremely anxiety-inducing. When we're too worried about ourselves and how we appear and whether others like us, the conversation becomes a performance rather than an experience to relish in the moment. We lose connection and spontaneity. We stop focusing on what matters: the other person, the connection, and the flow of the conversation.

For those of us who have struggled with social anxiety or shyness, it can be a revelation to realize that **we don't actually have to change who we are as people to succeed socially.** In fact, what matters is trust, openness, genuine respect, curiosity, kindness, and validation–all things that we are already capable of.

How to make the switch

Simply reminding yourself to switch your focus can work wonders. But there are other things you can do, too. Let's take a look:

Tip 1: Cultivate genuine curiosity

It can be stressful to keep wondering, "What should I say next?" Instead, relax and ask a question. Be genuinely curious about the person in front of you and ask open-ended questions that will inspire more than a generic response.

While it's almost always a good move to ask a question in a conversation, a really thoughtful question also communicates an additional message: "I find you interesting. You're important enough that I find myself wanting to know more. Could you show me some of the things you know?"

Merely asking the question at all is validating and keeps your focus on your conversation partner. A great idea is to also pay attention to their nonverbal expression and energy levels. Notice when something seems to excite or interest them, then ask a question about *that*.

"So, what made you decide to move?"

"If you could have as many dogs as you wanted, how many do you think you'd go for?"

"What advice would you give to people wanting to do the same?"

Tip 2: Reflect and react

It's not a "conversation" at all if two people are merely standing next to each other, taking turns to talk in the other one's direction! A living, dynamic conversation is one that is a one-time co-creation of both participants. That means that your role is to truly listen to what you're told, process it, add something of your own to the idea, and hand it back to them. If two people can repeatedly flow through this pattern of listen-process-return-process, then what emerges is a conversation that's bigger than the people who are having it.

Be engaged and responsive. Don't be afraid to let go of what you thought the conversation was going to be, and wherever possible, avoid going back to old ground just so you can say something you've been internally rehearsing. Listen, then reflect what you've been told. "Oh, wow, how interesting! So you mean you don't technically *own* any dogs, but you've always fostered?"

This shows people not only that you're paying attention, but that you care about really comprehending what they're saying. You can then take things further and add something of your own. "Sounds interesting. Is it difficult when they're rehomed, though? I wonder what it's like to have them for such a short time..."

Tip 3: Limit self-referencing

You don't have to be a martyr or a doormat to be a good conversationalist. Naturally, a big part of authenticity is showing up in conversation as the person you actually are. That said, try to limit attempts to actively steer things back to yourself. Too much of this leads to "conversational narcissism," and the other person may feel as though they can't speak without you making it all about yourself.

Really, there is seldom any need to relate things back to your experience at all. For example, if the person you're talking to loves dogs and is enjoying telling you all about them, enjoy the conversation without trying to squeeze in the fact that you also have a dog, or that you're allergic. You can be fully present and participate happily in a conversation without being its focus.

Chemistry through playfulness

I don't need to tell you what chemistry is–you already know, right?

Nobody can quite explain it, but we all know exactly what it feels like. That alone is a powerful clue about the nature of chemistry: it's not something we can easily talk about intellectually or pin down. It's something we *feel*.

Now, in talking about chemistry, I don't want to give the impression that I'm only concerned here with romantic attraction. I believe that interactions of *all kinds* can be characterized by their unspoken "energy" and overall vibe, and if we want to be more charming and likeable conversationalists, then we need to figure out how to work with this energy.

In the last section, I explained how important it was to shift your understanding of what conversation really is, and how to reorient your attention and focus away from yourself and to the other person. Yet even though you might be able to chat comfortably with someone, it's not quite the same as having that sizzle, that *chemistry* with them. So, what's the difference?

Dr. Wendy L. Patrick is a trial attorney, behavior analyst, and the author of *Red Flags: Frenemies, Underminers, and Ruthless People. According to Patrick*. She believes that chemistry can be explained by this simple formula:

Rapport + Positive tension = Chemistry

Rapport is the general positivity, warmth, understanding, kinship, comfort, liking, and trust between people. Now, that's all very nice, but is it chemistry? According to Patrick, no. For that, we need to add a sprinkle of tension.

Positive tension is anything outside of the norm that makes us sit up and pay attention. It is the feeling of being ever so slightly off balance, the introduction of something unexpected, the allure of the suddenly unknown, or even a tiny amount of embarrassment or shock. In other words, the addition of a *small* amount of positive tension is what makes things feel fun! This is the magic ingredient of playfulness, and it's what transforms "nice" conversations into conversations with chemistry.

Following the formula, we can create chemistry by fostering rapport–and then throwing a playful spanner in the works to create just enough tension to make things interesting. Again, we don't need to relegate this trick to dating. Humor, wittiness, liveliness, and being a little unexpected can all bring a breath of fresh air into any conversation.

Being fun and light-hearted quickly builds intimacy and connection, and lowers stress for everyone. It also builds trust over time and acts as an invitation to become more comfortable together. After all, when people "play," they are effectively saying to one another, "I don't see you as a threat. I'm not a threat, either. So... let's have fun?" When people are disarmed in this way and they put their guard down, they are far more available for real connection.

Chemistry peps people up and tempts them to engage more. It encourages a mood of creativity, honesty, and authenticity. Plus, one often forgotten function of chemistry is its almost magical ability to defuse tension and cut through conflict. Playfulness melts judgment and suspicion. We'll explore conflict resolution at the end of our book, but for now, know that a well-timed joke and a bit of playfulness can smooth over a world of tension and awkwardness.

The rules of the game

The vibe of an interaction instantly changes when you think of conversation as a game, and not as a competition, performance, lecture, or otherwise. But even games have rules. Here are some to keep in mind when bringing more playfulness into conversations:

Be appropriate

Sexual playfulness is obviously verboten for professional or platonic situations, and we need to pitch our humor correctly, to avoid causing offense. Always remember that the goal is not to make you look clever or funny, but to create a playful atmosphere that everyone can enjoy. That means that if the other person is not in the mood for playfulness, then there's just no point trying to force it.

Amuse yourself

With the caveat about appropriateness aside, here's something you might find surprising: being playful in interactions is not so much about thinking of something that other people will find amusing, but rather just... amusing yourself. Young children understand this instinctively. They seldom invite others to play; they simply start playing, and other children are naturally attracted to the game, and drawn by curiosity to what looks like fun.

Trying to entertain others can quickly distort the dynamic and bring in pressure and obligation. Instead, just have fun, and notice how quickly other people become interested in joining you.

***Rapport* comes first, not tension**

If you introduce playful tension before you've established rapport, you risk coming across as awkward, creepy, disrespectful, or desperate. Rather, the surprise introduction of tension works precisely because it happens against a backdrop of trust and comfort. Without that backdrop you just have... tension.

Talk about things you have in common, share experiences, even throw in a compliment or two (more on that later) and *then* playfully add in a little tension. You can do this by offering a lighthearted challenge, a little light teasing, an unexpected comment, or a slightly off-the-wall joke. The rapport should make up the bulk of your interaction, with a tiny amount of tension sprinkled over it.

Make it fun for everyone

It's simply not the case that you have to be mean, edgy, or a little rude to make a good joke or come across as witty. Instead, keep focusing on ways to create fun and enjoyment for both of you. Outright jokes aren't necessary either; you can create a very strong atmosphere of fun and humor without having people rolling in the aisles. Ask people fun "would you rather" questions or make a mildly embarrassing admission about something unexpected that you like. If you're a master at inverse charisma, you'll have no problem with a little clowning now and then!

What playfulness looks like

Keeping the above rules in mind, what does it actually look like in a real-life conversation to be playful and build chemistry?

Given that we already know that chemistry is more of a feeling than something you can read about in a book, try to read the following examples with an open mind. Written down, what follows might not seem especially playful or fun, but delivery makes a big difference and is difficult to capture in black and white.

As you go out into the world and attempt to bring a little playfulness in your own conversations, remember playfulness often comes down to that elusive "energy," body language, facial expression, and most importantly, the genuine desire and ability to enjoy yourself and the other person. This is simply not something you can fake!

With that caveat in mind, what follows are a few examples of "playfulness" in the wild. See if you can identify what exactly might make them effective.

- You're visiting someone in their home and they make a joke and start apologizing for the meal, saying they're a terrible cook. You laugh and say that of course they're not, the food is delicious… and then, in a rather camp and theatrical voice, you announce that even if their cooking is so bad it ends up killing you, it would be an honor to die in such fabulous company.
- You're at a professional conference and catch someone's eye. "I'm only here for the free snacks," you laugh, as though revealing a juicy secret. "What brings you here?"
- While having a friendly chat with a group of acquaintances, you playfully rope in someone who's been a little quiet. "Yikes,

Sarah, these guys are ganging up on me. Come to a guy's defense?"
- In a work meeting with colleagues that you know very well, the boss announces, "There's good news and bad news. The bad news is that because of the renovations next door, none of us can get in here to work tomorrow." You quickly say, with a big grin on your face, "Wait, are you sure that's not the *good* news?"
- A friend takes one look at your daring pink and orange Hawaiian shirt and raises a single eyebrow. You say, "It's a little thing called *fashion*, Greg. Don't worry, it's not contagious."
- You're paying for a ski mask at a small sports store. You're having a friendly chat with the cashier when she asks you who the mask is for. "Oh, it's for me," you say nonchalantly. "I was thinking of robbing a bank this afternoon." She laughs and says, "Oh? How exciting! Well, just so you know, if you get caught there's no refunds!"
- Someone says to you, "Hey, will you promise you'll take a look at that paper later?" You give a devilish smile, rub your hands together and say, "Oh sure, I can *promise* you whatever you want…"

As always, try to keep in mind the rules of the game and the formula, namely that **Rapport +**

Positive tension = Chemistry. Think of positive tension as a light sprinkling of seasoning on top of a good healthy serving of rapport. A little goes a long way.

Remember that you don't have to stress about finding something extremely clever, funny, or interesting to say. If you don't quite manage to pull it off, that's OK! *Relax*, lean into it, and enjoy yourself, and the playfulness will come with time.

Mastering conversational receptiveness

Being "open-minded" is a little bit like being a better-than-average driver. Everyone seems to believe this of themselves, even though it's statistically impossible! We may truly believe that we are open-minded and willing to have genuine conversations with people on all sorts of topics, but if we examine ourselves more honestly, this open-mindedness may be little more than the willingness to patiently explain to others why they're wrong... or else ignore them entirely.

The world is more complex, noisy, and fractious than ever before. Debates (or should we say arguments, battles, and all-out *wars?*) seem to be held at a rageful fever-pitch, especially online and in the media. Patience, grace, and genuine understanding are more or less absent.

Even when we're not actively butting heads with someone, there may still be a subtle attitude of being more or less closed off to what the other person is expressing, and a feeling of inflexibility or unwillingness to accommodate them in any way.

Julia Minson is an associate professor of public policy at the Harvard Kennedy School of Government. Her research is in the area of conflict, negotiations, and what she calls the "psychology of disagreement."

For our purposes, Dr. Minson's work can reveal interesting insights into how to engage with people who are different from us. (Hint: That's just about everybody!) Though she focuses on hot-button topics like politics, race, and identity, her theory about "conversational receptiveness" applies to all of us, whether we're dealing with high-stakes conversation topics or not.

Minson says, "**Conversational receptiveness is specifically using language—words and phrases—to convince your counterpart that you are paying attention and thinking hard about what they're saying.**" (Nerenberg, J. 2024. "How to Turn Down the Tension in a Conversation" in *The Greater Good Science Center at the University of California, Berkeley*).

According to Minson, it's not enough to merely be receptive to the other person's perspective; you also have to actively *signal* that receptiveness to them via your body language, and the words and phrases you use.

Thankfully, it's not rocket science. Phrases like "I get you," "I understand," or "I hear what you're saying." are like gold dust in conversations, even when there isn't any conflict or disagreement. Let's take a closer look.

The HEAR acronym

The **HEAR acronym** is useful and easy to remember when you're in the middle of a conversation:

H is for Hedging: This is when you soften and moderate what you say with words like maybe, might, some people, sometimes, possibly. Instead of saying something like, "This is the only way forward," you could say, "In my experience, I believe that this is a great way forward, and I think that may be the case for some other people, too." We'll explore the power of language to diffuse conflict in more detail in Chapter 5.

E is for Emphasizing Agreement: You do this by using words that show that you and the other person are on the same side. Simply using "we" instead of "I" does the trick, as would a phrase like, "we agree on XYZ," or "I also think/feel...." This is simply highlighting agreement and areas of commonality, rather than focusing on everything that is not aligned.

A is for Acknowledgment: This is where we make efforts to show that we've heard and understood what they've told us, either through paraphrasing, reflecting, or straight repetition. The best acknowledgment is not just a recognition of the literal words you've heard, but a sincere attempt to grasp the deeper meaning and intention behind that person's perspective, even though it's not your own.

We want to show that we understand their point of view *as they themselves understand it*, not as it looks through our own lens of perception. For example, if someone calls themselves "pro-life" and frames their opinion this way, we acknowledge them by using this same label, rather than our own, for example, "anti-abortion" or even "anti-woman"–labels which will inevitably create tension, rather than resolve it.

R is for Reframing to the Positive: This is a gentle tweak you can make to change language that may inspire resistance into something more positive. For example, instead of saying, "That's weird, I can't imagine ever agreeing to something like that," you could say, "I think I'd be interested in hearing a bit more about the alternatives." This step could be as simple as finding gentler, more euphemistic replacements for words that act as triggers for more disagreement and defensiveness.

The great thing about using Minson's HEAR method is that it's contagious. The more conversational receptiveness you can show, the easier it is for other people to show you that receptiveness, too. **If you can maintain an attitude of genuine warmth, respect, and curiosity, the other person tends to reciprocate**. If, on the other hand, you're bringing an energy of defensiveness, superiority, or hostility, it won't be a surprise when the other person reflects that same attitude back to you.

People who possess an innate conversational genius understand that **it's not really *what* you say, but *how* you say it.** You communicate more through your own energy, attitude, and style of communication than you do with the literal ideas and concepts you put forward verbally.

Have you ever had a conversation with someone who you instantly took a dislike to, even though it would be difficult to say exactly why? They may have said all the right things, and ticked all the right boxes, but somehow you still didn't like or trust them. This is what happens when people make rational-sounding arguments and appear to be polite and intelligent–but the emotional engagement is missing. What may also be absent is a real feeling of *receptiveness* from their side.

In Julia Minson's research, a particular linguistic style was associated with conversational receptiveness. But it's likely that this style is just the external manifestation of a deeper attitude of genuine respect, curiosity, and openness to the person in front of you.

The next time you find yourself in conversation with someone different from you, or someone you might ordinarily fail to find any common ground with, try to keep the following in mind:

Disagreements and differences don't matter. Truly. You can make enjoyable, generative, and illuminating connections with people of all kinds. Though people can bond over similarity, it's not a necessity. In fact, realizing that you can learn something from everyone you meet is a big step towards cultivating an attitude of real receptiveness.

Focus on the vibe, the emotional undercurrent, the connection, the mood, and the energy *first*. Once you have that nailed down, every discussion you have can be interesting and productive. Without it, you will find a way to disagree even with people you agree with!

Set your ego aside. It's hard, I know. It is essential to prioritize connection, understanding, and even fun, above the need to be right, or the need to have others agree with you.

Hold it all gently. There's room in the world for millions of different perspectives, and it's always an option to simply refrain from stating your opinion, choosing a side, or making your perspective known. Just be comfortable with the ambiguity and stay open, rather than trying to forcefully decide who's right, who's better, or who's winning.

Reduce your exposure to "conflict bait." If receptiveness is an area of difficulty for you, one practical thing to do is cut down on the amount of time you spend online or engaging with social media. These platforms are specifically designed to encourage and exacerbate conflict and rage, and can teach unhealthy mental and emotional habits. Instead, go out into the world and talk to real people.

Assume the best. Be charitable to people and give them the benefit of the doubt. For example, if you don't quite understand them, rather than assuming that they don't make sense, assume that you simply don't understand yet, and keep asking questions.

Minson's work has been utilized to facilitate conversations around challenging topics like vaccines, gun control, and religious topics. Typically, her work has been embraced by people on one side of the political spectrum in an attempt to manage and handle objections and upset from people on the "other side." But one way to think of conversation, however, is to drop this "my side" and "their side" mentality. While Minson's work has been used to resolve tensions and conflict, to encourage people to adopt certain policies, or to resolve certain cultural tensions, the truth is that **when we think of people as being on the "other side," we have**

already lost a big chunk of our conversational receptiveness.

We do not use the HEAR framework to gently coax people around to our point of view, but rather to disarm our own egos so that there is as little as possible getting in the way of a genuine connection with them. **Make connection and real engagement your goal**. Expect that there *will* be something to bond over and be receptive enough to engage with it when it happens.

Quiet listening vs. loud listening

Let's revisit the two tasks mentioned by Julia Minson above:

1. Be open and receptive
2. *Show* that we're open and receptive.

The same thing can be said to apply to the more specific skill of listening. We need to not only actually listen, but also demonstrate our listening, for the other person's benefit.

If you've ever spoken to someone who was dead quiet and unresponsive as you spoke, you'll understand why "loud listening" can be so important. If the other person is listening but there is no external indication that they're listening, the overall effect is as though they weren't listening at all.

Loud listening is:

- Listening with your body and reflecting the emotional content of what you hear in your own nonverbal expression and body language. For example, when they smile broadly or frown, we smile or frown too, and if they lean in, we lean in.
- Acting like a "conversational cheerleader," supporting and encouraging the other person to tell their story. This is a little like being an attentive and engaged audience. You say, "Really?" or "Uh-huh," or "Wow, then what?" These are not interruptions, but rather supportive interjections that maintain focus and attention on the speaker.
- Show receptiveness, interest, and even gratitude for what you're told. People communicate because, on a deep level, they want to be seen, heard, and validated. They want their story, their experience, and their perception to find a place in the world and to be received as though they have value and belong. You can communicate all this to them by showing your full attention, and saying things like "I'm all ears," "t=Tell me everything," or "Ooh, now *this* is interesting!"
- Be sincerely curious. Ask meaningful follow-up questions that show you're paying attention and that you want to

know more, and explore what's being shared with you in an open-ended, unrushed way. Walk into their world. Don't be in a hurry to get to "your turn."

Loud listening can strengthen connections, build trust, increase rapport, and bring more energy and dynamism into an interaction. When you listen loudly, you bring energy and liveliness into the room and into the conversation. Your interjections and short questions act as playful spurs and prompts to encourage the person to talk more.

When a conversation is characterized by loud listening on *both* sides, it can be energizing, fun, and a great back-and-forth. It's a surefire way to communicate to people that you care about them, you care about what they have to say, and you're not going to hijack or derail the conversation to center yourself.

All that said, loud listening is sometimes... well, too loud.

This kind of listening may not work for a person who comes from a culture where *any* interruption of a speaker is considered rude. Different cultures have different conversational rules, men and women may differ in their preferences, and there may also be subtle variations between age groups or even personality types. What's more, loud listening may work in some situations and contexts, and not in others.

Let's look at another option: quiet listening. This type of listening may be more familiar to you, and is all about using silence to create an opportunity for people to talk and open up. It's just as "active" as loud listening, but the activity we are talking about is consciously *creating space* into which the other person can share.

When we engage in quiet listening, we dial up our presence and focused awareness, but dial down our own expression. We take a step back and just listen. We still make a few quiet noises such as "Hmm," or "Uh huh," to show that we're alert and present, but this is minimal. We might ask a question, then wait quietly while we give them time to answer, without rushing in to offer something else or give our own opinion.

As you can imagine, this kind of listening is best suited for more sensitive conversations, in-depth topics, longer interactions, or those where emotions are running high. This is the kind of listening you might experience in a counsellor's office, or any time you have something heavy on your mind and you just need to unburden yourself.

Now, quiet listening and loud listening both have their place. The real art and skill comes from knowing when and how to use each of these tools in your listening inventory. Listening is always a good move, and few of us will go wrong if all we ever do is listen more and speak less. But our conversation skills will improve dramatically if we learn to discern the best *way* to listen.

Feel out the connection first

The simple goal of listening is to make sure the other person is (and feels) heard, understood, and accepted. The goal of listening is *not* to give a good performance of being a good listener. After all, if you're so busy giving the impression of being a good listener that you've actually stopped listening, then there's a problem! The right way to listen is the way that best suits the other person's style of communication, as well as the overall context and atmosphere of the moment.

When you listen to people, listen to *all* of them. Try to get a sense of why they might be talking, what their emotional need is, and what they may be hoping to get from the conversation. If you imagine that your role as a listener is to help the speaker share their message, it will become clearer which style of listening will be most appropriate. It's often enough to simply note the initial energy level in the interaction; if the person is quiet, still, and slow, they may appreciate more quiet listening. If they're more animated, outspoken, or actively seeking your eye contact and engagement, then they may prefer loud listening, instead.

Let your body do the talking

The distinction between "quiet" and "loud" is an oversimplification. Have you ever noticed that some people can walk into a room and dominate the conversation without saying a word? Or have you noticed how some people can talk and talk and talk, and yet they seem to make no impact at all?

Literal silence can be warm, inviting, and active. By the same token, constant chatter can also feel lonely or empty. All of this is to say that we need to think bigger than silence vs. making noise. Remember that when it comes to communication, you have a rich palette that goes beyond the words you speak. You have body language: facial expressions, postures, gestures, nonverbal sounds and expressions, the way in which you move, the speed and manner in which you move, eye contact, proximity, and the way you position yourself relative to the other person.

Instead of thinking just in terms of whether you make noise or not, try to support and feed the other person's expression through both verbal and nonverbal channels. Nod your head and mirror their expression. Return eye contact. Lean in a little as though to say, "Tell me more," or lean back as though to say, "Wow, that's unbelievable."

Notice any bids for a certain type of listening

If you pay attention and listen carefully, you may sometimes notice that people willtell you what kind of listener they want you to be. If a person is regularly saying things like, "Right?" or "Don't you think?" and looking at you expectantly, it's safe to assume that they are making space for you to jump in and support them with some loud listening. "Oh totally!" or "I agree. What happened next?" would be responses that demonstrate you're aware of that need and are happy to fill it.

On the other hand, if someone is not reaching out in this way to engage with you, they may be communicating that they just need to find their own words and express what's on their mind without interruption.

Finally, be mindful of context

Loud listening is best for causal or impromptu conversations that are not about anything in particular. These are relaxed and friendly conversations between equals who are not in any rush. Read the room and if most people appear to be engaging in this kind of listening, follow their lead. Quiet listening is usually best suited for formal, planned, or unusual situations that require more forethought, or have a deliberate spoken or unspoken agenda.

Key takeaways:

- There are many misconceptions about communication and good conversation skills.
- One valuable mindset shift is to cultivate inverse charisma, i.e., to work harder at making other people feel valued than we work at making them see our value. When you can make others feel like they are captivating, interesting, valued, and well-regarded, you automatically make them like you more anyway.
- People largely enter into conversations because they want to connect and feel seen, and as such, your listening and validation is likely more important to them. Shift the spotlight from yourself and learn to center others.
- Cultivate a spirit of trust, openness, genuine respect, curiosity, kindness, and validation. Be interested in others, limit self-references, and actively listen and reflect.
- Chemistry is a feeling and not an idea. We can use the following formula to help us deliberately build it: Rapport + Positive tension = Chemistry. Build rapport first, be appropriate, and make sure everyone is having fun.
- Consistently remind yourself to practice real open-mindedness and intellectual humility, being as receptive as possible to other perspectives. Conversational

receptiveness requires communicating our receptivity to others both verbally and nonverbally.
- The HEAR acronym is helpful: By Hedging your comments, Emphasizing agreement when possible, Acknowledging what your conversational partner is actually saying,, and Reframing for the positive, we can truly connect despite our differences. Maintain an attitude of genuine warmth, respect, and curiosity, and the other person will likely reciprocate.
- Finally, understand the difference between quiet and loud listening. Use the former when presence and creating space are more important than encouragement and engagement.

Chapter 2: Overcoming shyness, nerves and insecurity

"Because true belonging only happens when we present our authentic, imperfect selves to the world, our sense of belonging can never be greater than our level of self-acceptance. Vulnerability sounds like truth and feels like courage."

Brene Brown

One of the *biggest* impediments to becoming a great conversationalist is not selfishness, an inability to listen, or being an uninteresting or uncharismatic person. Rather, it's **anxiety**.

When we are anxious (or shy, nervous, insecure, introverted, or whatever other word we can use to describe it) we enter into social situations with an attitude of fear, rather than curiosity. This fear displaces any genuine interest, playfulness, or compassion we might ordinarily bring to the table.

Luckily for us, learning to manage and release anxiety is one of the most reliable ways to make sure we are more emotionally available in social situations. When we are relaxed, our field of perception widens, we become kinder and more generous, and we are able to explore, learn, and play–socially, that is.

The 10-second conversation trick

One way to relieve nerves and tension before socializing? Rehearse and practice ahead of time. Charles Duhigg is the author of *Supercommunicators* and he explains his 10-second technique for preparing to enter any social situation. The idea is simple: you **plan ahead and think of three topics that you can talk about should the conversation fall into a lull**.

The idea is not necessarily that you'll need these emergency topics, but rather that you'll feel more relaxed knowing they're there. That sense of relaxation itself is often enough to ensure you naturally don't run out of things to say!

Try to think of the last time you felt anxious about an upcoming social situation. Maybe it was meeting new acquaintances, attending a work meeting or function, going on a first date, or even just making small talk with a long-lost uncle at Thanksgiving dinner. Chances are that a lot of your anxiety came down to a few thoughts and worries:

What am I going to say?

What if we end up having one of those awkward silences?

What if they ask me a question and I just draw a blank?

Now, first things first: while these are legitimate fears, the truth is that in natural, connected conversation, they seldom spell disaster. However, worrying about them in anticipation *is* a problem, since it pulls our attention and awareness away from the other person and onto ourselves. This can even create a horrible feedback loop or cycle: because we are worried about awkwardness, we actually behave in ways that are awkward... which only makes us worry more!

Duhigg's technique is a way out and takes just 10 seconds. He claims to have been inspired to try this trick by Alison Wood Brooks, a professor and researcher who also specializes in the fascinating realm of human conversation. Brooks believes that people tend to behave more confidently and calmly when they have a few pre-prepared conversation topics at hand.

Topics can be anything you like, but examples include current events, sports, a new movie or TV series, an interesting event that has recently happened to you, something exciting that's coming up, a funny anecdote, or an idea you've been thinking about. You can keep your topics very broad, or narrow them down a little, perhaps even thinking of a specific anecdote you can share, or a question you might like to ask.

Then, when you're in your social situation, remind yourself to take a deep breath and just enjoy yourself. Rest assured that you have something to "pull out of the bag" if necessary. A few more pointers on this approach:

You likely won't even use your topics

Think of these topics like the spare tire in your car. You probably won't need it, but it feels so much better knowing it's there.

"Most of the time, you won't actually discuss those things, but your anxiety levels will go down considerably because you feel like you have something to fall back on," says Duhigg. "If there's an uncomfortable silence, you know exactly what you're going to bring up... and the more calm and relaxed we are, the easier it's going to be for us to really connect with someone and have a great conversation." Ironically, the more that happens, the less need you'll have of your back-up topics.

Preparation allows for spontaneity

Sometimes, socially anxious people can attempt to forcefully control every aspect of an interaction to try and manage the stress they feel... with disastrous results. Trying to control and steer every aspect of the conversation will kill its flow, and nothing will create awkwardness more than the other person realizing that what you are sharing has been carefully prepared and rehearsed ahead of time.

Duhigg's trick is not about this kind of control; rather, it's about doing a small amount of work in advance precisely so you can be freer and more spontaneous in the moment. While identifying some topics in advance is a great idea, you are not rehearsing anecdotes word for word, nor will you be trying to find a place to squeeze in your pre-prepared sentiments.

Prepare questions

It can be frustrating to speak to someone who is clearly just waiting for the right opportunity to say what they want to say, regardless of whether the conversation is there or not. Asking a question is almost always a better move than making a statement or sharing some insight or opinion of your own–especially if you're trying to get out of a conversational dead end or lull (Huang et. al., 2017, "It doesn't hurt to ask: Question-asking increases liking").

It could be as simple as, "Watched anything good on TV lately?" or "What's your plan for the weekend?" Admittedly, these are not the most thrilling questions in the world, but they will get you out of a pinch and have the conversation flowing again. With a little more preparation, however, you can devise more interesting questions that are tailored to the other person. Ask about their work, their life, their pets, their family, their habits, their plans, or their likes and dislikes.

Duhigg claims that "supercommunicators" may ask up to ten or twenty times as many questions as other people when having a conversation, and that this is a big part of why they come across as more interesting, likeable, and confident. Another trick he says is part of the supercommunicator skillset is the ability to be keenly aware of body language and nonverbal communication, and also to mimic and reflect that to communicate a kind of understanding and empathy.

If there is an awkward silence...

Even with the best preparation in the world, people are all unique and entirely unpredictable. **There *will* be times that conversation lulls or splutters out–and that's entirely normal!** Even skillful communicators will find certain conversations hard to start up, and that's OK. It certainly doesn't mean that anyone is doing anything wrong, that a mistake has happened, or that anyone needs to feel ashamed or worried.

Preparation is important and will go a long way towards soothing pre-socializing nerves. That said, we also need to go easy on ourselves and accept that there will always be a degree of unpredictability and vulnerability whenever we encounter other people. The truth is that a slightly awkward silence is not the end of the world.

If you find yourself in a conversation that is struggling or you're in the middle of a weird silence–try to stay calm! Your reaction is what matters. You don't need to rush in and say something profound or get in a fluster in an attempt to avoid it or pretend it's not happening. Try to remember also that there is another person in the experience with you, and they might be finding the moment tricky, too. Smile, stay as open and relaxed as possible, and ride it out. If you can, find a little humor in it, but rest assured that a little awkwardness never hurt anyone.

Speak up!

Take a look at some of the following statements and see which, if any, you agree with:

- Your chances of being liked are higher if you speak less and listen more
- It's best to hold back a little on strong opinions, in case you make people uncomfortable, or even worse, they judge you

- The best conversationalists are those that don't hog attention and speak too much, but rather listen

Now, in the previous sections, we've explored at length the power of listening, receptiveness, and inverse charisma. "You have two ears and one mouth," right? By de-centering ourselves, we can open up to truly hear and understand people, and appreciate their perspectives.

However, there is an enormous caveat to all this: **routinely speaking less or holding back in conversations is *not* associated with greater likeability.**

A 2022 study in the *Personality and Social Psychology Bulletin* (Hirschi et. al., "Speak Up! Mistaken Beliefs About How Much to Talk in Conversations") explored two broad psychological tendencies–the **reticence bias** and the **halo ignorance effect**. These two psychological tendencies may stem from a good place, but they ultimately mean that we misjudge the ideal ratio between talking and listening.

Do we want to be perceptive, respectful, curious, and focused on the other person? Absolutely. But we also need to balance this with opening up and revealing a little of ourselves. If anxiety and shyness are ongoing issues for you, these two biases may be more pronounced–which means you may need to work a little harder at pushing against them.

The reticence bias

The word reticence refers to a kind of bashfulness, reservation, reluctance, or restraint. Basically, it's anxiety. When we are reticent, we hold back. And what exactly are we holding back? Ourselves.

The reticence bias is the unwillingness to share of ourselves in conversations, usually for fear of judgment or rejection. This may go along with the belief that if we hold back and behave ourselves, then others will like us more. We may have plenty of insight to share, and loads of thoughts, feelings, and opinions, but keep these back because we believe there is no place for them. However, some studies actually show the opposite. **People are found to be more likeable when they talk for at least half of the conversation.**

But isn't it polite, and kind, and nice to listen more? It may be, but the truth is that being reticent is not really about politeness or kindness at all. When you keep quiet and hang back, it may be more accurate to say that it is a *defensive* move, and a result of an underestimation of your social abilities. Again, this comes from anxiety, not politeness, and it's certainly not for the other person's benefit. In a way, we are judging and rejecting ourselves before anyone else even has a chance to have their own opinion, and we're assuming that others will do the same. We may automatically assume that others will respond to us worse than they will.

Anxiety is also at the root of what's called the "liking gap," which is the difference between how others feel about us, and what we guess they feel about us (i.e., we assume they like us a lot less than they do). As is characteristic of anxious communication styles, **reticence can be a self-fulfilling prophesy,** and a vicious cycle. Many socially anxious people may worry deeply that "People don't like me!" And yet those very same people, if asked, might say something like, "Like her? We don't even know her. She seems nice, but she does keep to herself…"

If self-minimizing, self-censoring, and keeping quiet are all a part of your coping strategy in social situations, then try to start gradually revealing a little more of yourself. Notice what happens when you do in fact share an opinion, a detail about your life, or your true feelings on something. Trust that others are interested in you and want to get to know and like you. Give them the chance to do this by opening up and letting them see the real you.

The halo ignorance effect

The other effect is called the halo ignorance effect, and it refers to **the tendency we have to**

change the amount of time we spend speaking depending on the goals we have for a particular conversation. In particular, we may end up speaking less if our goal (conscious or unconscious) is to be accepted and appear more likeable.

However, if our goal is to come across as interesting or intriguing, then we may be tempted to speak more. The study's authors say, "People recognize that they should speak more because, perhaps intuitively, people might realize they cannot be interesting if they are not saying much; they need to contribute more substance to engage the other person and capture their interest."

The trouble is that this estimation is entirely inaccurate–people *don't* tend to separate likeability and interest in the way we assume they do. We don't tend to like people more if they speak less, or find them more interesting if they speak more. Rather, research shows that we tend to form an overall impression of a person based on our interaction with them as a whole.

Just as with the reticence bias, we mistakenly think that talking less is more likeable. In actual fact, we tend to like people who are contributing actively to an interaction, bringing energy and positivity to the conversation, and engaging naturally and comfortably. In other words, in real life it goes far beyond "talk less" or "talk more," and is all about *how* we engage, and how we make others feel in conversation.

Knowing that there is a risk of *under*estimating the ideal speaking time, you can make efforts to correct both of these biases in your own conversations. The good news is that these changes are often more comfortable and enjoyable anyway.

We need to push back against the mental narrative that tells us that good conversationalists are meek, quiet, and repeatedly keep themselves back from the interaction. Don't confuse being a good listener with being someone who doesn't talk much. (As we've seen in a previous section, listening can be very loud and active indeed!) Be generous not just with your attention, but also with your energy, and your contribution… in other words, be generous with sharing your unique self.

Tip 1: Try to speak for at least half the time

Airtime and attention are not gifts that you have to sacrifice for the other person in order to convince them to like you. The conversation is a shared experience where you are both welcome (and required) to participate as the people you are. Naturally, you don't want to blurt out deeply sensitive secrets or truly controversial opinions to someone you barely know, but trust that it's OK to be chatty, to share yourself, and to say what you think and feel. People like people who share!

Tip 2: Balance listening with sharing

Listening is a wonderful and necessary part of conversation. But it's not the only part. While some of us struggle to reign it in and curb our conversational narcissism, others will need prompting to put ourselves out there a little more. Finding the balance isn't some complicated mystery; just be alert to the fact that you can mix sharing with asking questions, listening with self-disclosure, and inquiring about opinions with sharing your own.

After you share a personal story, ask the other person about their life and invite them to share a story. If they tell you something interesting or share an anecdote, respond to it and then offer something of your own in return. As long as the interaction is warm and respectful, you'll build more rapport than if you had merely sat quietly and listened.

Tip 3: Don't be afraid of self-disclosure

Think back to the last genuinely interesting person you met. What made them so interesting? Chances are, the most memorable part of the interaction was when they shared something unexpected, something different, or even something you found strange or disagreeable. Don't be afraid to reveal yourself authentically and lean into all those things that actually make you different from the norm. It's ironic that often, people actively conceal the most fascinating parts of themselves and work hard to portray a more generic, sanitized version of themselves to others. Of course, we all want to know the real version, not the "nice" fake version!

The old self-help classic *How to Win Friends and Influence People* contains Dale Carnegie's original advice for getting people to like you: talk less. "The people you are talking to are a hundred times more interested in themselves than they are in you," he explains. That may be true, to an extent. However, if anxiety and shyness are a problem for you, it may be more productive to invert this advice, and instead understand that the whole point of conversation is to *connect*. There are two people in a conversation, and you are one of them. So don't forget to show up!

Three levels of conversation

Have you ever shown up somewhere and suddenly realized that you were dressed completely inappropriately? You thought it was a certain kind of event but really, it was another. Oops.

Well, the same kind of misunderstanding can happen in conversations, too, and it can be just as awkward and confusing. If you hit the rewind button on many awkward, strange, uncomfortable, or somehow "failed" conversations, you may identify the problem: the people involved were actually *having two totally different kinds of conversation,* or else having the same conversation at two different levels.

The "three levels" concept was first introduced by Douglas Stone, Bruce Patton, and Sheila Heen, and appears in their 1999 book *How to Discuss What Matters Most.* As the title suggests, the book is all about navigating tricky interactions, but it also has plenty of wisdom for helping us avoid weird misunderstandings in the first place.

According to Stone et. al., conversations can be separated into three broad types or levels:

1. The "What happened?" conversation
2. The feelings conversation
3. The identity conversation

The problem comes when we don't appreciate that not every conversation is the same, and that the two people talking may in fact have different assumptions about the overall purpose of their conversation.

The "What happened?" conversation

The purpose of this conversation is to establish and clarify the facts–usually facts that have occurred at some point in the past. So, someone might ask, "Hey, I see there's no milk, have we run out?" and someone might reply, "Hm, we must have. Let's pick some up later."

Though simple on the surface, this kind of conversation can go wrong for a few reasons:

- We assume that our assessment or perception of the facts is the only one that exists, or that it's right
- We differ in our interpretation of the facts
- We misunderstand people's intentions, and think that we're being attacked, or
- We get stuck trying to figure out who's to blame... all the while overlooking the factual details of the situation

Returning to our example, someone could respond to the innocent question, "Hey, I see there's no milk, have we run out?" in a few unhelpful ways:

- "There is milk, you're just not looking properly." (They have different facts.)
- "It's no big deal, I don't know why you're complaining." (They have different interpretations-is the person really complaining?)
- "Don't look at me, I never even use milk." (They get defensive, assuming an attack.)
- "Maybe *you* used it up and didn't get any more?" (They try to assign blame)

As you can see, "What happened?" conversations tend to fail when people don't realize they are, in fact, in a "What happened?" conversation and leap ahead to their own conclusions, assumptions, and interpretations. Arguments can quickly follow because people then start to react to these interpretations. The facts (the whole purpose of the conversation) disappear as people get distracted by irrelevant details.

The feelings conversation

The purpose of this conversation is to communicate how we feel. It's important to note that this level does not mean talking about things with feeling, but rather talking about feelings themselves. Sharing our emotions can sometimes feel risky because we are opening ourselves up to rejection, misunderstanding, or not having our needs met. Carefully conveying feelings is a lot more difficult and nuanced than conveying facts, which can be expressed in simpler and more concise language. Naturally, conversations about emotions can also be difficult because some emotions *are* difficult–for example anger, shame, disappointment, sadness, and so on.

Here's an example of a feelings conversation: Someone sits their partner down and begins to explain that they are feeling frustrated and unappreciated because they feel that the other is not doing their fair share of housework. This kind of conversation can go wrong when:

- We respond to their feelings with logic, rationality, or an attempt to problem-solve on a superficial level.
- We ignore the emotional content entirely.
- We invalidate, punish, or reject the feelings being shared with us.
- We hear the expressed emotion but respond to it indirectly.

To follow through with the example, you might hear the other person's frustration with your inability to do your fair share at home, and respond by saying:

- "OK, fine. So we just need to get a cleaner or something." (You offer a factual response and attempt to problem-solve.)
- "But I do clean up. I took the trash out yesterday." (You are ignoring emotional content.)
- "I'm sorry I'm not perfect and can't meet your high standards. But if you're going to be so difficult, I'll take a day off tomorrow and clean the house top to bottom, would that finally make you happy?" (You are engaging in invalidation, punishment, etc.)
- Or, you could simply avoid the conversation and quietly start doing your fair share, but without verbally communicating anything. (You hear the emotion and their request, but respond to it indirectly.)

The identity conversation

This level/type of conversation may be relatively less common. Its purpose is to communicate issues around identity. This can be a little more subtle, but our example will illustrate. Let's imagine that the ongoing conversation around household chores and cleaning is actually a deeper question of roles, identities, and values. Perhaps one believes that it's the other's job (i.e. identity) to clean, whereas the other resents doing it because it doesn't really align with their values, principles, or self-image as a decidedly non-domestic person.

Identity conversations go wrong when:

- One or both parties feel that their sense of identity is threatened or challenged.
- One or both parties are directly or indirectly making an assessment about the other's value or worth as a person.

For example, if someone says, "We're out of milk," the message they may *really* be communicating is, "I'm reminding you that getting the milk is your responsibility, and is part of your role/identity." This may be fine if the other person agrees with this identity assessment… but you can probably see that if they don't agree, conflict is inevitable.

Likewise, if someone says, "Oh no, you forgot to get milk again…" they are undermining the other person's value and worth; or at least, it may feel like they are! Any time people feel like their competence, goodness, value, relevance, lovableness, honesty, virtue, etc. is on the line, conflict and argument are not far behind.

Now, in real life you'll be talking constantly about thousands of things, at all different levels, for different purposes, and with different stakes attached. We all plunge into these conversations without ever confirming their deeper purpose or confirming that we are both actually having the same conversation. When you think about it, it's amazing that we don't fall into conflict and misunderstanding more often!

To make use of this 3 levels theory, we can glean a few key insights:

- We need to be aware that not all conversations are the same, and we need to pay attention to discern exactly what the purpose of a conversation is, and the level at which it's being held–not just for ourselves, but from the other person's point of view, too.
- We need to be open to the other person's perspective and perception, and work with it, rather than trying to correct it or forcefully bring them around to our own perspective or perception.
- Think in terms of appropriateness, rather than right vs. wrong or victim vs. villain. Before you can even have a conversation,

you need to agree on what the frame of that conversation will be. Be flexible on that!
- Be "conversationally agnostic" and don't make assumptions. Abandon your position and stay open-minded, seeking first to understand them, then to be understood.

Keep an open mind and ask yourself,

What kind of conversation might this be? At what level are we talking?

Is this person primarily concerned with communicating facts, feelings, or identity?

What assumptions am I coming into the conversation with? What purposes and goals do I have?

Are we aligned? Are we engaging in the same conversation?

Now, this is not to suggest that you delve into angsty overanalyzing every time you make a bit of small talk. In reality, the above questions can be done mentally in just a few seconds–all that's required is that you pay attention and take a moment to really consider where the other person might be coming from. Once you've determined the kind of conversation you're having, here's how to handle each type:

At the facts or "What happened?" level

Stay curious and keep your ego and defensiveness out of it. Adopt a neutral mindset, like a scientist or a journalist only interested in uncovering the truth, and what the truth looks like to the other person. "Here's how I see it. Can you explain to me what you're seeing on your side?" Use plenty of paraphrasing to reflect and confirm understanding, "So you're saying XYZ, have I got that right?"

At the feelings level

Whatever you do, don't ignore the emotions, even if they're difficult, confusing, or if you don't share them yourself. You can acknowledge your own feelings without making them mean anything about the other person's feelings. Adopt a compassionate attitude, create space, and avoid judgment or invalidation (i.e. suggesting that their emotions are somehow weird, wrong, mistaken, or otherwise illegitimate). Don't get tempted to bring in facts. Instead, use plenty of listening, questions, and emotion labelling.

At the identity level

Be aware and respectful of people's identities, roles, values, and principles. Tread with care and remember that you don't have to agree or understand–just acknowledge. "Hey, I know that you're an honest person and you always have been, so I would never suggest that you're lying."

"I can see that it's important for you to be the mediator here, and I can appreciate that."

When you understand that people communicate for a reason, and that they are relatively predictable reasons, you become a more skillful and perceptive conversationalist. The more you understand how to talk with people *in the conversations they're really having*, the more confident you'll feel about your own social skills, and the less impact anxiety and shyness will have over you.

From shallow to deep

One final cause of conversational anxiety is often a lack of confidence around *navigating depth*. Are you one of those people who hates small talk? Do you dread social interactions because you find polite chit-chat inane and inauthentic?

If so, then realize that this attitude itself can be a significant roadblock to becoming a good communicator. **The truth is that small talk does not get in the way of big talk; rather, small talk and chit chat are precisely *how* we warm up and work our way towards the big talk.** In other words, if you want to enjoy deeper, more meaningful, and richer discussions with people, the path that will get you there is the path of small talk.

While many of us crave deeper and more authentic communication, we may actually lack the skills needed to connect this way, and may even sabotage ourselves by deliberately keeping conversations shallow. What's more, if we demonstrate the reticence bias and assume that we need to keep quiet and hold back, we may repeatedly find ourselves in conversations that peter out. It's not because small talk is boring, but because we are unwilling to take the risk of deepening the conversation.

Depending on our upbringing, our personalities, and our cultural background, we may bring a certain hesitance to conversations. While it's normal to be a little reserved around strangers, if we consistently fail to underestimate how interested others are in our lives, and if we miss cues to go deeper, we may lose out on all those deep and meaningful conversations that we actually want.

Getting to know people is a process–it moves along gradual steps and stages of growing intimacy and closeness. Knowing how and when to move from superficial chat to more meaningful discussion is a skill, but in this section we'll discuss a useful technique that can make it easier.

Vertical vs. horizontal questioning
As we've already seen, questions–almost all kinds–are a great way to engage and show that you care and are listening. However, some questions will lead to a deepening of

conversation, while others will keep you skimming along the surface.

Vertical questioning is the kind that probes for depth. It's a question that invites the other person to dig a little deeper into one particular thought, feeling, or idea. A *horizontal question* keeps the conversation at the level it is, and simply switches the focus.

This does not mean that horizontal questioning is bad and vertical questioning is good, however. Both have their place. Horizontal questioning uncovers facts and interesting information, expanding the map of potential areas of engagement. Vertical questions can then be used to explore each of those areas in more depth.

A few examples will illustrate.

You might be chatting with someone at a work event, and, over the course of small talk, you ask them closed questions about where they went to college and where they grew up. After some time, you pick up on one of these areas and ask a vertical question. Recalling that they said they grew up in X place, you could ask them an open-ended question about something specific and slightly more personal: "Do you ever miss X?" or "Wow, that's interesting. What was it like growing up in X?" Notice how vertical questions often (though not always) move from facts to feelings.

Here are a few more examples of an initial horizontal question followed by a vertical one:

- "Are you feeling better after your car accident? It sounded really scary, what was it like for you?"
- "What did you study in college? What do you think made you choose that line of work?"
- "Did you have a good trip? What were your favorite parts?"

When you consistently pair horizontal with vertical in this way, not only are you ensuring that you never stagnate at the superficial level, but you will automatically come across as more attentive and thoughtful, because your questions naturally follow on from one another. In real conversation, you may find yourself working through this step-by-step, using questions that invite more and more depth revelation. Bear in mind, again, that as you're asking others to reveal a little more of themselves, you should be matching your own level of self-disclosure with theirs. That way, you are mutually enjoying a deep conversation, rather than just interrogating them!

When you ask vertical questions, you are inviting people to share a little about their feelings, their motivations, their interpretations, their preferences, their beliefs and values, their goals, and their history. You need to do this gradually, little by little. Trust is built not just by asking people to share something of themselves, but by responding with respect and care to what they share.

To show the power of vertical and horizontal questions in action, take a look at the following conversation, and see if you can identify exactly why it's sputtering out. Imagine that this is a first date between two people who have until now only exchanged texts and messages.

Him: "Wow, it's pretty cool we're finally getting to meet after all this time. Thanks for coming out."

Her: "Oh, of course, it's good to meet you in person. Sorry about bailing on you last week, I hope you understand."

Him: "Yeah, no problem. So, remind me what you do for work. You're an estate agent, right?"

Her: "Uh, no, a mortgage advisor actually. But I used to be in real estate, yes. You?"

Him: "Well, I'm finishing up my post-doc. Chemistry. I'm working with this amazing startup right now, we'll see how it goes…"

Her: "Oh wow, that sounds interesting. So, are you from around here?"

Him: "Yep, born and raised. I spent a few years in X though, back in undergrad."

Her: "Oh, really? I'm from X originally."

Him: "Yeah? You go to school there?"

Her: "Uh huh. X University. Came over here around 5 years ago."

Him: "Cool. Thinking of going back ever...?"

We'll pause the conversation here. Are you asleep yet?

While this interaction is perfectly pleasant and flows well enough, let's be honest: it's not going anywhere. Why? You may have noticed the distinct lack of vertical questions–despite there being several opportunities to go a little deeper. Both people keep asking closed, horizontal questions, and so they fail to move things along. This leads to a boring, question-response rut that lacks all chemistry and fun. If you hate small talk, it's this kind of inane back-and-forth you're likely thinking about. Let's take a look at how different it could be:

Him: "Wow, it's pretty cool we're finally getting to meet after all this time. Thanks for coming out."

Her: "Oh, of course, it's good to meet you in person. Sorry about bailing on you last week, I hope you understand."

Him: "Yeah, no problem. So, remind me what you do for work. You're an estate agent, right?"

Her: "Uh, no, a mortgage advisor actually. But I used to be in real estate, yes. You?"

Him: "Well, I'm finishing up my post-doc. Chemistry. I'm working with this amazing startup right now, we'll see how it goes…"

Her: "Oh wow, that sounds interesting. A startup, huh? What's that like?" (Here's the first vertical question.)

Him: "Honestly, it's too soon to tell. They're awesome people, but it's a *lot* of work."

Her: "Haha, I bet."

Him: "I'm giving it a year to see how we do, but there are loads of things I'm interested in, so it's all good."

Her: "Hmm, that does sound good. It's always good to have options."

Him: "Absolutely. What about you? What made you make the switch from your old career?" (The second vertical question, referencing an earlier response.)

Her: "Well, huh… that's a tricky one to answer! What can I say… maybe I just wanted something more challenging, you know?"

Him: "Challenging?"

Her: "Yeah. I think I get bored if things are too easy."

Him: "OK, got it. I'll do my best to make sure this date is as difficult as possible!" (And here's a little "positive tension" to create some chemistry.)

These two interactions take roughly the same amount of time, but the second has direction, and gradually moves from the superficial to the more personal. You can see that vertical questioning doesn't necessarily lead to heavy, overly-serious conversations–in fact in this instance, it's the depth that is giving the interaction its lightness and energy. It's also not necessary to have too many vertical questions for them to work their magic; it's more about gradually pacing the interaction so that it *unfolds*, rather than merely plods along from one thing to the next.

If you find yourself floundering in a shallow conversation, throw in a (thoughtful) vertical question and see where it takes you. Start with a few horizontal questions, then follow up with meaningful open-ended questions that ask people to share a little more. The trick is to do this gradually, comfortably, and in a meaningful way. And when someone responds warmly to your vertical question, offer a little self-disclosure in return so that you join them on the next level of depth.

Key Takeaways:

- A big impediment to authentic communication is anxiety and insecurity. We need to learn to release social anxiety and replace it with curiosity, so that we are more emotionally available in social situations.
- One easy trick takes just 10 seconds: Plan ahead and think of just three topics that you can talk about, should the conversation fall into a lull. Silences now and then are normal and nothing to be afraid of. Ask a question to get things flowing again.
- While listening is good, research suggests that routinely speaking less or holding back in conversations is *not* associated with greater likeability. The reticence bias and halo ignorance effect may make us speak less and hold back; instead, we should strive to share ourselves, speak up, and be authentic.
- We tend to misjudge the ideal ratio between talking and listening, or assume that speaking less will make others like us more. Don't be reticent, and aim to speak for about half the time, sharing your real self. Balance listening with sharing.
- There are three levels of conversation: the "What happened?" conversation, the feelings conversation, and the identity conversation–each according to their

assumptions and purpose. Be clear about which conversation you are actually having to avoid conflict and misunderstanding. Is this person primarily concerned with communicating facts, feelings, or identity? Check your alignment.
- If you find small talk difficult, make better use of vertical questions to gently encourage people to share more intimately, and to create trust and connection. Horizontal questions, on the other hand, tend to keep conversations where they are.
- Small talk does not get in the way of big talk, it actually enables it. Getting to know people is a gradual process that leads towards more intimacy and closeness. Remember to match their revelations with your own self-disclosure.

Chapter 3: How to speak so that people can hear you

"There is no greater power on this earth than story."

Libba Bray

You may consider yourself a fairly good listener and nice enough company when it comes to small talk, but do you break out into a cold sweat at the thought of having to tell a joke? If you're one of those people whose stories and anecdotes always seem to flop or fizzle out, this chapter is for you.

Telling a good yarn, relating an amusing anecdote, or explaining in three simple sentences what work you do–all of these require the ability to present what is, essentially, a story. Being a good storyteller takes time and practice, and it's not a skill that comes naturally to many of us. However, with a few tweaks and adjustments, you can begin to speak in ways that others instantly "get" you.

The mystery of the Jennifer Aniston Neuron

In a 2020 paper titled "Universal principles justify the existence of concept cells" was published in the journal *Scientific Reports* (Tapia et. al.). In this paper, researchers found fascinating and convincing evidence for the theory of *concept neurons*. Over the past few decades, neuroscientists have wondered at the precise way the brain stores and processes unique memories and ideas. One of the prevailing hypotheses is that each and every concept you can think of has its own cell or neuron.

So, for example, the musical note A or the concept of the actress Jennfer Aniston or the idea "my grandmother" all have their own dedicated neurons. In fact, this is sometimes called the "grandmother neuron" hypothesis for this reason. The 2020 study used complicated mathematical modelling to test–and verify–their theory, undermining the competing theory that abstract concepts in the human mind are a result of the activation of complex neuronal webs.

Valery Makarov, Senior Researcher of the Fundamental and Applied Research Department at the Centre for Translational Technologies, explains it this way:

> *"A key role in the brain is played by neurons, the nervous system cells that are*

> *responsible for receiving, processing, storing, and transmitting signals. Currently, a common opinion prevails in science that the emergence of abstract concepts in the human brain requires complex, perfectly orchestrated interaction of myriads of neurons. However, there is a hypothesis that suggests that single neurons, the so-called concept cells, may be responsible for complex tasks performed by humans. These are individual neurons that form abstract concepts based on specific stimuli to which they respond, for example, the name of a human being. Thus, earlier the 'Jennifer Aniston neuron' was discovered, which fired whenever the portrait of the actress appeared on the screen. Such neurons that respond to the presentation of some image[s] are called 'grandmother cells.'"*

What's more, developments in electrode technology at UCLA now allow scientists to actually see the activity of individual neurons at work in the brain. Researchers here observed that particular neurons consistently respond to visual images of the same person–in their research, one example was Halle Berry, the American actress. They experimented with different representations, sometimes showing just her name, or only her recognizable outfits without displaying her face, or some other isolated visual elements that may make a person think "Halle Berry." The researchers did indeed find that certain neurons reacted to *all* of these variations, as though it were the concept itself that activated them, rather than any particular stimuli.

Neuroscience researchers now believe that understanding more about concept neurons will enable them to gain more insight into the workings of human memory. You may be wondering, what does all of this have to do with becoming a better conversationalist?

Concept neurons give us insight into how the brain creates coherent memories, and how it processes meaningful narratives from disparate concepts about people, places, and things. **Knowing how concept neurons work gives us a window into the way the brain takes in and processes information–and that's a big deal when we're thinking about how to communicate, listen, and talk so that people can really hear us.**

The brain during a conversation

The billions of neurons in your brain are hard at work during even the most ordinary of conversations. Their job is to take all the many different pieces of information, all the different stimuli coming their way, and craft a coherent whole from them. It's not just about processing bits and pieces of data and information–it's also about synthesizing complicated webs of social and cultural *meaning*, of sifting through memories and associations, and connecting it all with a good dose of shortcuts and guesswork.

For example, someone may casually mention a celebrity, a recent event in the news, a well-known cultural meme, or even a memory of a shared event from the past. Maybe they say "Mr. Darcy," "Taylor Swift," or "North Korea." Instantly, the other person's brain activates all the neurons it has that are associated with those concepts (if indeed it has these neurons). The very same process probably happened to you just now, when you read those words yourself!

Really, **this is the essence of communication: if people can hear one another's prompts and connect meaningfully to the concepts they're sharing, they will naturally feel as though they understand one another.** Knowing that the words coming out of your mouth have successfully activated just the right neurons in the listener's brain leads to feelings of connection, engagement, and satisfaction.

When the process works, conversations feel like they flow well, and we find it easy to empathize, to get on the right wavelength, and to see exactly where someone is coming from. Lots of good vibes and rapport are now possible. When the process doesn't go quite right, however, there may be awkwardness, misunderstanding, or this nagging feeling that the other person doesn't quite *get* you.

Knowing that there is a real neurological basis for this "click" of connection between people, what can we do to improve the chances we connect in this way?

Step 1: Begin by identifying a unique and shared concept

When you're getting to know someone new, keep your ears pricked for a unique and distinctive concept that you can grab a hold of–it's even better if this concept is also meaningful to you. People who are naturally sociable tend to do this without thinking, and can zoom in on things that are unusual, interesting, or otherwise seem emotionally important to the speaker.

This could be a hobby, interest, image, idea, memory, or interesting little detail. For example, you might notice the fact that your conversation partner is proud of an oil painting they managed to get displayed in a nearby art gallery. When you identify such a concept, make a mental note of it. You could also ask a few thoughtful follow-up questions about it throughout the course of conversation (you'll recognize this as the vertical questioning strategy).

Step 2: Create a memorable association

Next, you want to deliberately link up this concept with another iconic cultural image, idea, event, or object. Linking things in this way will make things more memorable for the brain and reinforce it as something relevant and meaningful.

So, in our example above, let's say the other person tells you, "Last month I was so thrilled– they finally agreed to show one of my pieces in the Ryerson Gallery. It'll be there all spring!"

You could note the concept, then respond by saying, "The Ryerson Gallery? Is that the place that has that really weird angel statue right in the front?"

Now, there are two links in your growing neural web of concepts. It's not only the concept neuron of "oil painting" which is being activated, but other neurons, such as those associated with the angel statue, the location in the front of the gallery, and so on.

Not only does this web of concepts make it easier to recall a particular idea, image, or memory, it also creates a strong shared feeling of connection between people, of somehow being part of the same world. In a very subtle way, mutually activating one another's concept neurons is a way that people bond and create feelings of agreement and similarity. The more activations, the greater the sense of bonding.

Step 3: Throw in a shared cultural reference

To reinforce the memorability of your growing web of concepts even further, you can weave in some broader cultural associations. By linking your conversation to wider cultural touchstones, you give the entire interaction more gravity, more permanence, and more context. The concepts neurons for these well-known cultural landmarks are "well-worn." By piggybacking off of them, it's almost as though you borrow some of their permanence and memorability.

In our example conversation, the other person may laugh and confirm that the Ryerson gallery does indeed have the "weird angel" statue out in the front. You could reply by saying something like, "I know that statue well, I go past it every day on my way to work. Kind of creepy though, don't you think? It always makes me think of something out of a Tim Burton film, you know?"

By sharing a cultural reference in this way, the conversation will instantly feel more real and relatable. Given this reference, can *you* imagine what the angel statue would look like? Even if you only have a vague idea, this mental picture creates anchors that you can return to in the future.

One caveat, however: cultural references can backfire if they're too specific or there's a chance the other person won't understand them, given their age or background. If someone doesn't understand a cultural reference ("Who's Tim Burton?"), drop it immediately and move on, otherwise you may end up creating feelings of disconnect.

People love familiar stories

Picture this: you're at home during the festive season and spending some time with your family. Your uncle on your mom's side is on the sofa, getting comfortable, and settling in to tell the story about your aunt and the runaway shopping cart from way back in 1992. *Again.* You know this story well because you've heard it dozens of times already, starting from when you were a child, and you can recite it from start to finish, including the punchline.

Now, you might think, "this guy has been telling the same old yarn for decades, he's definitely *not* what you'd call an engaging storyteller..." But, according to a new Harvard-led study, you'd be wrong. The researchers of this study found that, despite the common belief otherwise (and the groans of your long-suffering aunt), people actually enjoy familiar stories more than they do novel ones.

It may seem natural to assume that the best stories are new stories, but this is only if we understand the purpose of communication as a kind of entertainment or at the very least an information exchange. However, if we see conversation in a different way, i.e. we understand that it's also about bonding, identity, connection, and comfortable familiarity, then we can start to appreciate the value of the same old same old.

The paper, published in the journal *Psychological Science* (Cooney et. al., 2017) explores the deeper function of storytelling in humans, and comes to the unexpected conclusion that **although people like to *tell* new stories, they like to *hear* familiar ones.** While a storyteller might work hard to make a tale seem new and interesting, the researchers identified what they call a "novelty penalty," namely that listeners actually have to do more work to process completely new information, and this additional work undermines and weakens connection. So, your uncle might be onto something.

Gus Cooney, one of the study's leads, explains,

> "It struck me that we always try to add these novel stories to conversations, and then it doesn't go over as well as we think and then conversations kind of naturally drift back towards talking about familiar things or things that we have in common with other people."

The study included 90 participants. Half were asked to be listeners, the other half speakers. The listeners then watched a video, and the speakers watched either the same video, or a different video. These speakers were then asked to relay a story about the video they'd seen to a listener. From the listener's perspective, then, the story they heard would either have been a new one, or one they had already watched themselves.

Surprisingly, the listeners rated the stories they already knew as more enjoyable–even when they predicted beforehand that they would like the new stories better. This means that while we may think that we like and value novelty more, in the moment, we actually enjoy what we find familiar.

Remembering concept neurons, we can see why: when we hear a story that we're familiar with, we can't help but add in our own memories and fill in the blanks with what we know. In other words, we participate and engage. The story feels like it's ours. By hearing the retelling of this piece of "shared mythology," we are instantly connected to the same context as the speaker, and this creates feelings of trust, kinship, and understanding. A new story, on the other hand, requires a lot more mental energy, and the payoff is not yet really known.

Cooney explains that the outcome of this study doesn't mean that we need to bebroken records that never share any new information at all. Rather, it's about striking a balance between novelty and familiarity.

> "In our study, when both parties had viewed the same video, if the speaker made a mistake about something in their story, the listener could just fill in the information since they had seen the same video [...] But when the listener hadn't watched the same video and didn't have that necessary background knowledge, it was very easy for them to get confused."

We need to respect the fact that the human imagination, though powerful, does have its limits. It can be quite fatiguing to have to keep track of a narrative stream of new people, places, events, and things. Neurologically speaking, it's easier and more enjoyable to activate existing neurons than it is to build new neural pathways. In this respect, clarity and brevity are always preferable, whether the story is old or new. People cannot be delighted with a story if they're too busy trying to figure it out!

Striking the new/old balance

Let's look at some concrete ways to apply this insight to our own everyday conversations.

Tip 1: Make the familiar your starting point

You can use familiarity and recognizable old stories to anchor an interaction, ensuring sure you're starting from a position of connection and relatability. When you establish your conversation on these foundations of familiar events, you build up a little bonding and rapport.

If you meaningfully connect the old with the new, it may be easier and more comfortable for the other person to follow.

Now, you don't need to be enormously close with the other person or have already shared plenty of experiences with them. A familiar story can also just be a universally recognizable human experience. You could lead up to your novel story by saying, "You know that feeling when you walk into a room and can't remember what you're doing there? Well, it was a little like that for me the other day, when I started my new job…"

Tip 2: Be strategic in how you add novelty

Novelty is not a bad thing; it's just "cognitively expensive," so it needs to be introduced in small, manageable chunks. When you add novelty, do so in bits and pieces, and take care to be *clear* above all.

From your perspective, you already know all the details of the story, how they fit together, and how everything comes to a resolution. But your listeners don't. They likely don't know all the information you're telling them, how long the story is, or what the point is. Be mindful, then, of their position and slow down, keep things simple, and make it relatable. You want to entertain and bond, not confuse.

Let's take a look at this story:

"So around 4 years ago, probably like the second big lockdown we went into, I was still with APS here in Richmond, and we were doing a program with a bunch of 504 students from up north. Terry Calhoun comes in and–this was on Thanksgiving weekend–he tells us all that we're being audited, and all hell broke loose..."

How would you feel being on the receiving end of this story? You're probably wondering what APS is, or who the 504 students are, and if the name Terry Calhoun rings a bell or not. Where is "up north"? North of Richmond? Where's that?

The words "audited," "lockdown," and "program" do make sense to you, but you might find yourself scrambling to see how they all fit together. All in all, the listening experience is strained, and you probably don't feel very connected to the speaker at all.

Now consider this version:

"Have you ever encountered something so ridiculous you were convinced that it had to be a joke somehow? Well, in my old career as a social worker, we worked with the strangest man I've ever met in my life. Now, his name was Terry, and one day..."

This is the same story, but told in a much more comfortable, relatable way. It's easier to engage with. Can you see the balance between familiar and novel? Can you see how this story is presented with plenty of consideration for the listener? Even tiny changes and adjustments like these can make an enormous difference to how well people feel they can connect with you.

Tip 3: Keep checking for engagement

Bearing in mind what we already know about active and "loud" listening, understand that storytelling is really a group effort. Unless you have an alert, engaged audience that is actively following along with you, you don't have a story at all. At best you have something like a monologue.

"Have you ever encountered something so ridiculous you were convinced that it had to be a joke somehow?" You can see that the question at the end is prompting and encouraging a response from the listener. Even if they don't verbally confirm it, they will be thinking, "Yes, I've had an experience like that."

If you pepper your stories with these kinds of prompts and questions, you get the chance to check that your listeners are still with you. Notice if they're nodding and smiling, or responding in other ways that show they understand the emotional impact of what you're saying.

If you do notice that they seem to have gone a little blank, or are no longer responsive, don't panic. Simply return to an earlier, more familiar part of the story. If you've laid solid and familiar groundwork, you'll still have the foundation of rapport that you need to connect, even if the details of the story need repeating or clarifying.

"Yeah, so do you remember what it was like in the early days of lockdown? How weird and unpredictable things were for a while?" Once you feel like the other person is on board again, you can continue the tale.

Asking follow-up questions

"The great question that has never been answered, and which I have not yet been able to answer despite my thirty years of research into the feminine soul, is 'What does a woman want?'"

These are the infamous words of psychiatrist Sigmund Freud, who, had he been a better conversationalist or in the habit of truly listening to his women patients, might have easily figured out a solution: just ask them.

When it comes to communication skills, charisma, and relationships, the socially anxious often ask very similar questions: What do people actually want? What do they like? What are they really thinking? The answer in this case is the same we could give to Freud: *Just ask them!*

Questions are conversational tools that we deploy not only for the benefit of the other person, but for ourselves, too. Asking questions helps us to engage and connect, and makes our interactions with others richer, more lively, and more meaningful.

In fact, there is now research to support the idea that **asking the right questions can increase your likeability in other people's eyes, as well as improve your overall emotional intelligence**. Harvard Business School professor Alison Wood Brooks and her research team ran a series of studies and concluded that people who ask questions learn more about the world and about others, and are better liked.

Their 2017 study, published in the *Journal of Personality and Social Psychology (Huang et. al.)*, analyzed more than 2,000 speed dating and online conversations. "In all 3 studies, we found that asking more questions in conversation, especially follow-up questions, increases interpersonal liking of the question asker," claim the authors, further explaining that, "those who asked more follow-up questions received more second dates and favorable impressions."

What is it about follow-up questions that creates these results? It is not really the mere act of asking a question; rather, **the follow-up question is an expression of the real secret ingredient: responsiveness to a partner.**

In the study, Brooks and her colleagues identified six kinds of questions: introductory, mirror, full-switch, partial-switch, follow-up, and rhetorical questions. They noted that in the observed conversations, about 44% of all the questions asked were follow-up questions. These are questions that, because they lead on meaningfully and thoughtfully from what has already been said, demonstrate the listener's real interest and active engagement. Questions are good, but follow-up questions are the gold standard. A follow-up question is a neat little package of empathy, listening, and attention all in one–not to mention it keeps the conversation flowing.

Of course, not every question is created equal, and we have to guard against becoming too lazy with our question-asking. As long as we keep reminding ourselves that the real value lies in demonstrating and expressing our interest, and our willingness to respond to the other person, then our questions will create more depth, fun, and connection.

Brooks warns not against any particular question, but rather against asking questions from the wrong attitude or mindset. For example, if we are driven to ask questions from a place of fear, egotism, or boredom, they likely won't land very well. At the same time, holding back questions out of doubt, apathy, or the fear of coming across as rude can be just as disastrous.

If we are overly anxious, unsure, or focused only on how we ourselves are coming across, then our questions will seem hollow and will not actually advance the connection or create any flow. Have you ever been in a conversation where the other person subjected you to question after question, never giving you a moment to return with a question of your own? There's a good chance that that person was quite anxious themselves and using questions defensively. All of this is to say that questions in themselves are neither good nor bad, but when they are an expression of true interest and engagement, they are like conversational jet-fuel.

According to Brooks, there are a few things we can do to master the art of the follow-up question, which will not only build our emotional intelligence, but better communicate that intelligence to others. (And hopefully, encourage them to find us totally likeable!)

Tip 1: Be intentional

There's no rule that you have to be completely spur-of-the-moment with thoughtful questions. You can set a specific goal for the number and kind of questions you'd like to ask ahead of time, before even beginning a conversation. As we've already seen, the idea is not to rehearse a verbatim script, but to have a few options to reach for when you're in the middle of a natural conversational flow.

You might decide on a certain theme or idea to ask about, or you can set yourself a goal for a particular number of questions to ask. For example, knowing that you will soon be having a conversation with an acquaintance at a function, you can mentally prepare yourself to ask about the holiday they recently went on, the health of their family member, or a follow-on question from something they mentioned the last time you met.

"Hey, I was wondering, how did it go with your kid's hockey game? Did they win?" If there is no previous conversation to reference, that's OK; just ask an open-ended exploratory question first, and then try to refer back to their response with all your subsequent questions.

Finally, you could also challenge yourself to ask, say, five follow up questions in the conversation. Whether or not you reach this goal, one thing's for sure: you will be hanging on to their every word, and *that's* what they'll notice.

Tip 2: Listen closely for "ins"

If you pay close attention, you'll be able to spot little cues that you can later follow up on. Imagine that, as people speak, their speech opens up before you like a wall of text, except some of that text actually contains interesting hyperlinks, images, and emojis. What you want to do is notice those hyperlinks and "double click" on them to learn more. The way you double click is to ask a pointed, thoughtful follow up question that says, "this looks interesting… tell me more about *this*."

You'll know a "hyperlink" because it will usually be accompanied by more emotion in the speaker, or a sudden change in expression. By noticing and responding to these cues, you show that you're paying attention, that you understand, and that you actually care about what you're hearing. You're right there with the speaker. Skip over these cues and ask an unrelated question, however, and the person may feel unheard or undermined.

In general, switch your focus from facts to feelings. For example, if someone is telling you about how they recently found a baby bird in their backyard and are now nursing it back to health, you might notice that their facial expression really lights up when they talk about the little sounds it made, and how relieved they were when it finally woke up after looking like it might die. That's your cue! "Wow, that's so cute. What was it like, to see it coming back to life?" or "I love baby animals. What do you think it is that makes them so adorable?"

If you don't register this little flutter of emotion in the story, you might miss it, and instead make a comment about one time *you* rescued a baby bird, or else ask a question about what kind of food they fed it, and how much. Neither of these things will destroy the connection, but why not have a much more interesting, heartfelt, and fun conversation instead?

Tip 3: Be moderate

Let's recall what we already know about balancing depth and breadth, as well as balancing questions with personal revelation. While questions do indeed keep things moving and show the other person that you are attentive and responsive, there are limits.

Try not to ask too many questions in a row, even really meaningful follow-up questions. Instead, make sure the conversation is even and has some room to breathe, by including plenty of "space" and by sharing a little something of yourself. After all, it's only by offering little pauses and silence that we give people the opportunity to respond to us, to steer the conversation or to contribute in their own way–for example, they might want to ask us a question!

You don't need to stress too much about what counts as balanced or not. An easy trick is to simply include a little of everything at once. For example, if the other person has mentioned their love for old and obscure comic books, you could say something like, "Ooh, I used to love comics as a kid… but I'm guessing not the kind that a collector like you would ever be interested in! I'm curious, are any of your comic books super rare?"

In just two sentences, you've reacted to what you've been told, you've made a mini revelation about yourself (along with some very slight self-deprecating humor), and you've asked a meaningful (and vertical) follow-up question. You have recognized their contribution, while making your own. The balance is maintained.

Incidentally, when you offer your own contributions in this way, people will seldom feel like you are dominating the conversation, and you won't get stuck in "tug-of-war" style interactions. Instead, things will flow. It will feel as though both of you are equally involved.

The case for spoilers

The title of a short report in *Association for Psychological Science* is "Story Spoilers Don't Spoil Stories." This title makes a pretty good spoiler itself since it is, in essence, what the paper is about!

According to a research team at the University of California, San Diego, (Leavitt & Christenfeld, 2011) we don't actually need to be all that worried about spoilers spoiling our enjoyment of a story. In Chapter 2, we explored the unexpected finding that old, familiar stories are in fact more enjoyable than novel ones, and in this chapter, we'll explore a related finding: **Stories are no less enjoyable when we already know how they'll end**. In fact, knowing the punchline, as it were, may actually make stories *more* enjoyable.

Various studies used more than 800 participants to hear and rate certain stories under different conditions; the consistent finding was that people tended to prefer the stories they already knew the outcome of. By this point in our book, you can probably guess why: Spoilers lessen the cognitive load of a story and make it easier to digest and process. Such stories are not only easier to follow, but the anticipation itself adds to the pleasure of hearing the story.

It's as though, in knowing what the destination is, people can simply relax and enjoy the journey to get there. We are happier to be surprised by the twists and turns along the way if we ultimately know where it all leads. This effect has been called *perceptual fluency*, and theorizes that when cognitive burden is reduced, the ease of integration increases, and along with it, enjoyment.

Other theories emphasize the "pleasurable tension" aspect of spoilers. After all, just because you more or less know what happens at the end, it doesn't mean you experience any less of the delicious anticipation that comes with waiting for it to happen. Knowing that something fun is on the way can build excitement and heighten focused attention. Just think of approaching a step drop on a roller coaster–knowing that it's coming doesn't take away from how thrilling it is when it does!

Whatever the exact mechanisms, how can we apply this insight about spoilers into our own conversations and storytelling? We'll look at some tricks below, but the biggest takeaway is to realize, again, that your job as a storyteller and conversationalist is not to entertain or impress, but *first* to connect with your listeners and create a feeling of flow, warmth, and enjoyment. Good storytelling does not require shock or novelty. A good conversation is not about the destination at all, but the enjoyable process along the way.

Tip 1: Hint and tease

People like spoilers, but that doesn't mean they have to be big ones. Offer a little sneak preview, almost like a trailer for a film. A small hint like this can ramp up curiosity and engagement, set the scene, and act as an emotional cue for the listener, so they can guess at what's coming up. This way, they can prepare and be waiting right there at the finish line for you.

Let's say you're telling the story of a hilarious camping misadventure. You start your anecdote by saying, "Did I ever tell you about that time Matilda had to sell her shoes to a guy at a farm shop in Tennessee? No? OK, well the thing you have to understand is…"

The whole time you tell the story, the listeners will be eagerly trying to fit every detail into the bigger narrative, and trying to understand how it all eventually leads to Matilda selling her shoes. This creates a curious kind of "in on the joke" feeling from the outset, so that it's almost as though moving through the anecdote is a collective experience.

Get people invested in the story. Throw in a bit of mystery, add some teasing and hints, and, if you're blessed to be in the company of other good conversationalists, you can expect some loud listening in return, and possibly some encouraging questions to spur you on.

Tip 2: Make use of recommendations

Whenever you recommend something to someone–let's say a book, a movie, a TV show, or whatever–add in some (careful!) spoilers and teasers to pique their interest. Instead of simply saying, "Oh I loved it, what a great book" you could say, "The ending was so out-of-the-blue, I'm still thinking about it now." or "When I read it I did think of you... and if you read it I'm sure you'll see exactly why!"

Naturally, you don't want to give obvious plot details and ruin the ending, but you do want to try and create a little buzz and mystery, which will build suspense that you can then use as conversational fuel. This is a particularly good tip for those of us who don't consider ourselves especially good storytellers–we can always piggyback a little on other people's stories.

Tip 3: Relax and slow down

It really is about the journey, not the destination. What makes a story captivating is not the resolution or punchline – in fact, this is just a small part of a story's anatomy. When it comes to building rapport, good vibes and connection, what matters is how you get there, how things unfold, and the atmosphere you build along the way.

Whether it's your own story or someone else's, you could say things like, "Well, as you can guess the guy gets the girl in the end, and they live happily ever after, but you would never guess *how* they got there…"

When you can, emphasize the journey and not the destination. Take your time and don't rush. Make sure you are giving enough attention to each emotional beat of the story, and not just racing ahead so you can reveal the conclusion.

Tip 4: Think in terms of tension and payoff

It would be a mistake to ignore the follow-up research that has since been done in this area. An article by Levine et. al. (2016) showed that our enjoyment of spoilers might be more complicated than it first appears. Their findings actually show the opposite of Leavitt & Christenfeld, i.e., that spoilers do indeed spoil.

What are we to make of this? On closer inspection, comparisons between these two studies suggest that the type of story matters, and that the type of spoiler matters, too. It may be that it's not really a question of spoiler vs. no spoiler that matters, but rather *how* a spoiler is conveyed.

In general, it appears that more nuanced, teasing spoilers were more enjoyable than blatant ones. Likewise, people may vary in their enjoyment of spoilers and hints, and their personalities may mean they prefer more or less cognitive effort for a story's payoff.

Rather than cling to any absolute rules, try to read the room and pitch your stories to match the context, the occasion, and the needs of the listener. If you're not sure, just pay attention. Note people's energy levels, attention, and enthusiasm, and adjust accordingly. If people are disengaged and bored, add a dash of mystery, tension, and a teasing spoiler that raises more questions than it answers. If they're already engaged, there's no need to torture them by making them wait for ages for the payoff.

Key takeaways:

- Storytelling is a big part of communication and good conversation, but it's important to know how to tell stories that people can really hear and connect with.

- Each and every concept you can think of has its own cell or neuron–a concept neuron. When you activate these neurons, people are better able to understand, process, and connect with what you're saying. Identify unique and meaningful concepts, make associations that will be memorable, and consider linking them to broader social and cultural touchstones. The more concept neurons you activate, the better.
- Contrary to popular wisdom, people actually love the retelling of familiar old stories, and enjoy them more than novel ones, which may require a greater cognitive effort.
- Neurologically speaking, it's easier and more enjoyable to activate existing neurons, than it is to build new neural pathways. Try to strike a balance between novelty and familiarity. Be clear, be brief, and consider the listener's perspective.
- Start with the familiar, and be careful and strategic with how you introduce the new. If in doubt, keep checking for engagement and revert to a shared concept if connection is lost.
- Asking appropriate and meaningful follow up questions helps us to engage and connect, making our interactions with others richer, more lively, and more

meaningful. Follow-up questions are an expression of responsiveness to a conversational partner.
- Finally, don't be afraid of giving little hints, teasers, and spoilers for your stories, since these may actually increase enjoyment.

Chapter 4: The tools of the trade

In the preceding chapters, our focus has been on the ideal attitude to have in order to cultivate better conversations, including various things you can say and do to best convey that attitude to other people. We then explored how to tell stories and anecdotes so that people could instantly enjoy, relate to, and connect with our message. In this chapter, we'll look even further at some of the conversational "tools of the trade," i.e. the practical skillset you can begin to develop in your own life.

Long and short pauses

We'll start with one tool that doesn't seem like a tool at all: silence. In the same way that the silences between musical notes are precisely what give the notes their meaning and character, silences in conversation are just as important as the words we do say.

We already know that silence is important because it creates literal and psychological space. This is a way to invite the other person's contribution and to demonstrate our active listening and attention. But silence has other functions, too.

A doctoral thesis by Kristina Lundholm Fors at the University of Gothenburg explored the role and function of pauses in human conversation. Specifically, Lundholm Fors wanted to understand how the *duration* of different moments of silence can impact a conversation. When we talk, we don't pause evenly after every single word. Also–listen carefully–we don't necessarily pause at the end of sentences where written punctuation might suggest. So, when do we pause? And why?

You've probably never noticed it before, but pauses serve multiple functions. They:

- Allow us to think and gather our thoughts.
- Make room for the other person to answer a question, interject, or share their own thoughts.
- Give us a moment to remember a detail or a word.
- Give us a chance to catch our breath!

In some contexts, silence can even be a form of purposeful communication itself, signaling for example refusal, acquiescence, uncertainty, respect, or curiosity. Lundholm Fors was interested in the length of pauses, but found that the question of "How long?" really depended on each person and each conversation. She noted that we tend to adjust our conversational pause length to accommodate the other person.

Lundholm Fors' research focused on eye tracking to monitor the way a person processes information. She asked participants to listen to different speech segments, then later asked what sentences they could recall. The results showed that speech delivered with unusually long pauses was harder to recall, suggesting that it was more cognitively difficult to process in the moment. Here, "unusually long" meant a duration of four seconds.

"Four seconds doesn't sound like a long time," she explains, "but when you are talking to somebody it can feel like an eternity. A typical pause in speech lasts only about a quarter to half a second."

Of course, pausing is a natural and helpful part of everyday speech, and the takeaway here is not to eradicate pauses completely. Rather, we need to be mindful of how and why we're pausing. Silence is not distributed randomly throughout speech, but purposefully, and *where* it occurs tells us a lot about the content of what we're hearing, as well as what we can call *meta-content*. This includes cues and signals about whose turn it is to speak, when the conversation is over, and a host of other pieces of information about how to actually structure the back-and-forth of a dialogue.

Lundholm Fors intended to use her study to inform the development of programs for people who struggle with communication, or to guide the development of language models. For our intents and purposes, however, we can use this four second threshold to make sure we're not unintentionally overloading our listeners and undermining our connection to them. Here are some ways we can apply these ideas.

Tip 1: Be mindful of how long and short pauses affect the listener

Long pauses can feel uncomfortable and disruptive. What's more, they may be perceived as hesitation or uncertainty on your part or, even worse, boredom. If the listener feels that even you yourself are not fully engaged with your own message, they will naturally find it hard to be engaged with it themselves.

Of course, you don't have to mentally count the seconds between pauses, but rather pay attention now and again to notice if you may be lingering a little too often or a little too long.

Short pauses increase the comprehension of your listeners and help them absorb what you're saying, all while maintaining the fluid flow of the conversation. It's a good idea to pause after especially important chunks of information or phrases, to allow people to catch up and process. However, these pauses can be surprisingly quick.

The best and most natural rhythm for pauses is one that best mirrors the meaning of the content. For example, try to read through the following and imagine the natural pauses you might insert.

"OK, so what you want to do is start at the main reception area, OK?... Go to the reception desk first, and get a map there... Once you've got the map, you can plan a route... But if you ask me the best hike is the 10 mile circular one... It's the red one... And you'll see plenty of signs marking the start of that route..."

Tip 2: Adjust your pauses as necessary

You might not have noticed it before, but each of us have a slightly different style and approach when it comes to the pacing, flow, and articulation of our speech. Depending on our upbringing, our background, our education, and many other factors, we may prefer to speak at a specific pace, overlap speech, or use pauses in our own idiosyncratic ways. Furthermore, every conversation is about something a little different, and takes place in its own context, meaning even as individuals we adjust the way we utilize pauses depending on what we're trying to achieve.

People naturally sync up with one another where pauses are concerned, but if a conversation is feeling stilted and uncomfortable, be mindful that it may be a mismatch in pause length–a problem easily solved by noticing and matching your own pacing to your conversation partner's. If you're with an elderly person, for example, you may need to make adjustments. Listen carefully, and consider adding more or slightly longer pauses so that you synchronize with their rhythm.

Tip 3: Use pauses to signal turn-taking

A pause can be a cue to tell the other person that you're done talking, and it's now officially their turn to speak. The silence acts as an invitation creating space for them to step into. You can be very deliberate about this, for example saying, "I love Italian. I was thinking we could book a table at that fancy new place. What do you think?" then pause. Or, you could be more subtle and let the pause itself act as a question: "I love Italian. We could book a table at that fancy new place…?" When paired with the right gestures and facial expression, this is as good as a direct question!

Troubleshooting

Silence and pauses are a little like air in a conversation. You don't really notice when they're doing their job, but when they're *not*, you know it instantly, and the conversation dies a quick death.

"If two persons involved in a conversation have different ideas about the typical length of pauses," Lundholm Fors says, "they will face problems with turn taking." And *that* means that you're at risk of misunderstanding, disconnection, or even creating offense. If you find yourself in a conversation where things feel a little awkward or clunky, take a moment to look at your pauses.

"Click" with someone through fast responses

So far, we've busted a few conversation myths:

- The way to be perceived as interesting is to make others feel that *they* are interesting.
- The way to get others to like us is not to be quiet, reticent, and cautious with our opinions, but to be forthcoming, to speak up, and even to bring in some "positive tension."
- The way to tell a good story is not necessarily to be novel, but to be familiar, even offering story spoilers.
- And finally, the way to capture and hold people's attention is not to slow down and deliberate, but to deliver information rather swiftly and without too much pausing.

If the picture we're slowly painting of the ideal conversationalist is not quite what you were expecting, you're not alone. In this section, we'll look at a couple more misconceptions, namely, the idea that interrupting people is always bad, and that polite, well-spoken people need to "think before they speak."

If you think of a carefully rehearsed TV debate, a dialogue in a film or book, or the kind of conversation held during a job interview, you can't help but notice that the turn-taking is deliberate and paced, i.e. people are careful not to talk over one another, and leave respectful pauses after one another. However, these kinds of formal and deliberate conversations are nothing like natural, everyday interactions.

According to Emma Templeton and her research team at Dartmouth College, **the speed at which people respond to one another in conversation is a great indictor of connection and rapport** (Templeton et. al., 2022, "Fast response times signal social connection in conversation." *Proceedings of the National Academy of Sciences*). In fact, this metric might be one that points to that mysterious phenomenon of "clicking" with someone.

According to Templeton, jumping in to share something before the other person is fully finished, or only just finished, is not really "interrupting," but a sign of being in sync, connected, and in the flow of the conversation. If you think back to your most enjoyable conversations, you might have already noticed this–there is an energy and swiftness to interactions. It's almost like you're reading one another's minds or finishing one another's sentences.

In Templeton's study, 66 participants were asked to chat to strangers for a short while–just ten minutes. Afterwards, each participant was asked to give a rating for how connected they felt to the other person, and to point to specific moments in the conversations where they felt the most rapport. It turns out that people rated their conversations as most connected and flowing when the response times were super short–even when there was no pause at all between what was said and its response.

Templeton et. al. concluded that quicker response times create feelings of connection. How quick? It turns out, pretty quick indeed: Senior researcher Thalia Wheatley says, "When people feel like they can almost finish each other's sentences, they close that *250-millisecond gap*, and that's when two people are clicking."

This effect runs both ways: When someone responds quickly to us, it is a demonstration that they are paying attention, engaged, and invested in what we're saying. They are responsive, and the energy and speed of that response becomes a proxy for the degree of rapport. On the other hand, we ourselves are more likely to respond quickly if we feel genuine interest or attention, or indeed want to show that to the other person.

Quick response times may create a positive feedback loop, amplifying feelings of connection.

Even more interesting is the variation on the study that Templeton and her colleagues ran: they asked others to watch recorded conversations and rate how well they thought the parties were connecting. The team manipulated the response times artificially, so that they were either sped up, slowed down, or kept the same. Across the board, uninvolved observers rated the faster response times as more connected. Conversely, slower response times tended to make people feel the connection was weaker and more distant.

Bear in mind that all the participants above did not know that it was response time that was under investigation–they were simply reporting their natural feelings about an interaction. Without being conscious of *what* was creating that feeling of connection, people nevertheless felt it.

Of course, response time is not the only factor behind a good vibe and a sense of rapport, but it certainly plays a role. Here are some ways to make the best of this aspect in your own conversations.

Tip 1: Be prompt, be natural

Let's be honest, most of us are not going to know how long 250 milliseconds (a quarter of a second) really is. But in natural conversation, neither will the other person. What matters is your swiftness. You might find that this rhythm is actually quite natural and spontaneous–if you're engaged, that is.

Don't worry too much about jumping in immediately with something interesting or relevant to say. It's the response itself that signals your interest and engagement, not the content of your response. So, if you can't actually think of any information to add, realize that you can still communicate plenty of rapport and attention by simply repeating or paraphrasing what you've heard, or offering an attentive reaction. For example, someone says, "Anyway, it's my brother's birthday today so we'll all head over later…" you can say, "Oh nice, a birthday! So you're going over there to visit him…"

In writing, the above looks like a non-response, but if delivered promptly and with genuine interest, eye contact, and warm body language, it's a perfectly friendly way to keep the flow going. Whatever you do, there's no point in forcefully holding back if you really want to respond.

Tip 2: Encourage them to respond faster, too

Templeton's research showed that it was prompt responses on both sides that created the best dynamic rhythm. You can subtly encourage the other person to respond quickly by matching and reflecting their energy and enthusiasm. Again, we are in "loud listening" territory. Together with plenty of open and receptive body language, little signals like this all send the same message: *I'm actively and eagerly awaiting your response.*

Tiny prompts like, "Ooh, tell me more," or "Really?" will help set the tone and cue the other person to reciprocate. Mirror their body language, vocal quality, and expression–and do it quickly. Without even realizing it, they may find themselves wanting to keep pace with you. If you've ever heard someone describe a person's enthusiasm as contagious–well, *this* is how you do it!

Tip 3: Practice "conversational pacing"

It's also worth paying attention to your partner's pace and matching it if you can. If you notice someone jumping in to respond fairly quickly, do the same–it will signal to them that you're on the same page, and you'll both be closer to "clicking." When people not only notice another person's energy and pace, but also mirror it, they send a strong message of connection and understanding that is felt on an almost primal or instinctual level. On the other hand, if you miss these cues and signals of engagement from someone else and fail to respond by picking up your own pace, it may have the opposite effect, and make people feel subtly unacknowledged or even rebuffed.

A word of warning before we move on: Fast reaction times do not mean blatant interrupting or cutting people off. Sometimes, we may jump in because we're *not* listening, and we're more interested in steering the conversation where we want it to go. Jumping in for the wrong reasons doesn't help foster rapport and can actually harm the connection we're working to build.

Quick responses build rapport and connection when they are felt to be honest reflections of one mind predicting, anticipating, and appreciating another. But a quick response that is merely seeking to override or dominate will obviously not be perceived this way. It's the same behavior, but inspired by two very different motives. We find ourselves where we were back in chapter 1: Mindset and attitude are everything. Start with genuine interest and attention and allow that energy to set the tone for the conversation.

The anatomy of a perfect compliment

When it comes to conversational tools, it's all about *how* you use them. Whether it's silences, pauses, spoilers, follow-up questions, or a little playful teasing, the art comes in knowing exactly when to deploy these tools, and in what way. Compliments are no exception.

Have you ever received a compliment that completely failed to have an effect on you? Perhaps you felt it was not genuine, and just a poorly disguised attempt to get something out of you. Perhaps it was phrased awkwardly or delivered in a strange way or at the wrong time. Perhaps it was not really a compliment at all, but a thinly veiled insult or judgment!

A single compliment can work like magical fairy dust in a conversation, but, sadly, good intentions and sincerity alone are not always enough. We also need to know a little about what a compliment really is, how it works, and how to give one properly.

Before we take a look at something like a "scientific compliment formula," let's be clear about what a compliment actually is, and the function it serves. We know that it's a great thing to listen to people, to pay close attention to them, to show empathy for how they feel, to ask them thoughtful questions, to be curious about their lives, and to genuinely want to learn a bit more about them as people. But *why* is all this a good thing?

Ultimately, communication of this kind is serving a deeper, more universally human need: the need to be seen, to be heard, to be valued, and to be appreciated. Yes, we communicate to share information, but on a primal level we reach out to one another to feel validated in one way or another. When this feeling of validation is intact, then we have a foundation on which to build cooperation, understanding, and conflict resolution.

One direct way to signal this appreciation for another person is simply to tell them we appreciate them! A compliment says outright, "I like you. You're valuable. I appreciate you." A well-placed and well-timed compliment can melt any resistance, ease understanding, and create real feelings of warmth and friendship. In general, people will communicate so much better when they feel appreciated. Also, they will be far more willing and able to hear and appreciate *you*. If you can indicate, even in a small way, that you are *interested in making your conversation partner feel good*, you are 80% of the way to creating a great connection.

In fact, in a study published in the journal *Neuron*, researchers used fMRI experiments to examine how the brain experiences certain rewards, concluding that "The acquisition of one's good reputation robustly activated reward-related brain areas, notably the striatum, and these overlapped with the areas activated by monetary rewards." (Izuma et. al., 2008). This means that social rewards, like feeling appreciated, valued, and praised, activate similar neurological structures as monetary reward. In other words, there may be some literal truth to the expression of "paying" someone a compliment!

Similar research (Sugawara et. al., 2012) suggests that compliments and praise are so beneficial for the brain it improves motor skill learning. The authors hypothesize that praise and compliments play a sophisticated role in motivation and incentivizing certain behaviors. It does not take complicated neuroimaging to understand that when people feel good about themselves, they will naturally feel more inspired to do more, more motivated to share and express themselves, and more willing to compromise and cooperate. This is exactly what makes for good communication!

A compliment is not just good for the one receiving it–the compliment giver also benefits. When we take the time to praise someone, we are adopting a more perceptive and appreciative mindset, actively looking for the good in people and in situations. What you focus on in this way expands in awareness. If you compliment a behavior in someone, it's almost certain they will try to repeat that behavior; in the same way, if you actively tell someone you appreciate that behavior, you are actually teaching yourself to notice and appreciate that behavior more. In this way, compliments are not about mere flattery, but act powerfully to draw people together.

Remember, not all compliments are created equal. Here are some ways to make sure your compliments are doing the trick.

Tip 1: Sincerity is everything

Of course, you should actually *be* sincere, but it's just as important to *seem* sincere, too. Truthfully, many of us are in the bad habit of giving completely hollow compliments in the misguided belief that we are being nice. We say, "Oh that's a beautiful jacket!" when really, we don't think it's beautiful at all, we've just noticed it, thought it was a good idea to say something, and the jacket was right in front of us.

Because real validation is so important, and sadly so rare, human beings seem to have a sixth sense for it, and almost all of us can tell a real compliment from an empty one given merely to be "nice." But it's better to be sincere than to just be nice. Remind yourself that a single genuine compliment is worth more than a dozen fake ones.

Tip 2: Be specific

"You look nice today." is lukewarm, even if you really do mean it. "Wow, those shoes are so interesting, they look fantastic on you!" is likely to be better received. The best compliments are specific–so specific it's like they're tailored precisely to that person and nobody else. Think carefully and ask yourself: What is totally unique about this person? Lots of people are pretty, or smart, or kind. Of course, these are great qualities, but you'll *really* make someone feel good if you praise something that is unique to them.

Tip 3: Compliment from their perspective

The compliment's job is to make the other person feel like a million bucks. That means it's worth complimenting something you know *they* value in themselves, even if that thing is not your particular focus. For example, you may notice that someone is going out of their way to make others comfortable in the workplace. You may not think any of it is necessary, and you may personally value all sorts of other things this person brings to the table. However, if you can recognize that this is what *they* value in themselves, then you can give a compliment like, "I love how attentive you are to everyone in the office. You're really good at putting people at ease, you know?"

Know how to take a compliment, too

Some of us have some pretty strange conditioning around compliments and praise. Without even thinking about it, we may respond to a compliment with instant resistance, downplaying or rejecting it. This reaction may come from a sense that it would be boastful or vain to "accept" nice words about ourselves, or it may come from low self-esteem. The fact is, however, that this behavior is just like throwing a gift back in the gift giver's face–it can leave *them* feeling unappreciated.

The best thing to do when you receive a compliment is to simply... receive it. Acknowledge that you have been praised, smile and accept the kindness and good intention behind it. Sometimes, it can be difficult to accept compliments if they contradict our own self-image. But switch this around and understand that rejecting a compliment is a little like saying the compliment-giver mistaken or wrong in their perspective. In any case, we can gracefully receive a compliment and the intention behind it without necessarily "agreeing" with it! Simply smile, make eye contact and say something like, "Thank you, that's very kind of you to say."

You don't have to argue, quickly change the topic, or think of a way to reciprocate–unless, of course, you genuinely want to.

How to structure a compliment

Compliments can be organized into four main types:

Appearance (example: "Wow, you look gorgeous in that dress!")

Skill (example: "You really have a knack for choosing just the right gifts for people.")

Possessions (example: "Nice wheels.")

Personality (example: "I really admire your creativity.")

A 1980 paper by Wolfson and Maines argued that English speakers tend to rely on a very narrow and predictable formula when it comes to compliments–and it works.

A great basic formula is:

Noun phrase + (looks/is) + (really) + (adjective)

This formula is especially useful for complimenting appearances and possessions. Take a look at these examples, with the noun phrase italicized:

"*Your hair* looks so healthy and shiny."

"*That paint color* is just perfect."

"*The way you speak* is truly inspiring."

Here's another compliment formula:

Pronoun + is (really) a/an + adjective + noun

Essentially, all the same content is present, but presented in a slightly different way. This format is great for recognizing someone's efforts, contribution, or hard work, making it great for professional or formal contexts. Here are some examples, again with the noun italicized:

"That was a delicious *meal*!"

"That was a really thought-provoking *point*."

"It was a beautiful *ceremony*."

One final formula:

You have a/an + (really) + adjective + noun

Naturally, this formula is best for complimenting personality traits and skills, but has wide applicability:

"You have a wonderful *sense of humor.*"

"You have a really tranquil *home.*"

"You have such well-behaved *children.*"

Pay attention to timing

Once the formula is sorted out, what about timing? Here are a few key ideas to keep in mind:

Compliment at the point of relevance

If you think of a compliment as a reward, then it's best delivered right after the "rewarded" behavior, so that the association is made perfectly clear. Offer kind words at the first bite of the lasagna, the moment you see the dress, or immediately after the beautiful ceremony. This will not only be more impactful, but will come across as more spontaneous and hence, more sincere.

Don't be inappropriate

Here are few times it's advisable *not* to compliment:

- In a serious conversation, particularly if the other person is upset with you or there is already awkwardness, a misunderstanding, or conflict.

- Outside of a natural conversation, or a pre-existing relationship. Complimenting strangers *can* be well-received, but it's best to reserve compliments for people you know, in contexts where they won't feel blindsided.
- Don't pair a compliment with a request, or it will seem like calculating flattery, no matter how sincere it really is!
- Try not to add in compliments to an apology as this may be felt to be manipulative.
- Avoid compliments about taboo subjects, like weight, sex appeal, or income.
- Finally, be mindful of certain gender dynamics. Between women, compliments about appearance are more appropriate and common, whereas between men compliments about possessions or skills are more usual. Between men and women, compliments are best focused on skill and personality; avoid compliments about appearances, as they might be misconstrued as flirtatious or inappropriate.

Compliment when it will be most impactful

If you notice the dinner party host seems nervous, compliment her at the *start* of the party so she can carry that confidence into the rest of the evening. Say a kind word to your colleague before they give an important presentation, or say something nice about someone's outfit as they're heading out the door to a first date.

Stay present, stay connected

One aspect of the stories and anecdotes you share you might not have considered before is their *tense*, i.e. whether your grammar indicates that the events happened in the past, are happening now, or will happen in the future.

This might seem like a pretty unimportant thing to dwell on–can such a slight grammatical change really make much difference? The answer is yes, absolutely! **The tense in which you deliver your message is yet another major variable that almost all of us overlook, despite it having an enormous effect on our engagement and perception.**

To prove it to you, consider the following two anecdotes, and imagine that they are being told to you by a person at a relaxed social gathering:

Anecdote 1: "The other day my husband and I were at home and this cute little song came on the TV, and he got up and started doing this silly little dance, right? But he pulled the zipper of his hoodie up like this, and I laughed and told him that strippers take clothes off, they don't put them on. You know what he said? He told me he was a *dyslexic* stripper!"

Anecdote 2: "So my husband and I are at home, and this cute little song comes on the TV. He gets up, and he starts doing this silly little dance. He's pulling the zipper of his hoodie up like this, and I'm laughing. I tell him, 'You do know that strippers take their clothes off, right, not put them on?' and he looks at me and he says, 'Well, I'm a dyslexic stripper then!'"

Now, the story is pretty funny either way, but can you see the very slight difference it makes to use present tense, as in the second anecdote? If you were hearing either of these anecdotes in real life, and you were asked to pick your favorite rendition of the story, you may choose the second, without quite realizing *why* you like it slightly more. In fact, this is pretty much what standup comedians have known for years, and have discovered through real-life testing of different versions of their jokes: **First person and present tense stories are almost always the most entertaining.**

It's grammatically correct and pretty normal to default to past tense when telling a story (he got up, I said, he laughed, etc.) but this may not be the most powerful, engaging, or rapport-building way to go about it. When paired with other storytelling skills, adopting the present tense can take a tale to the next level.

Researchers Sam Maglio and David Fang conducted a fascinating study where they analyzed millions of Amazon product reviews. The reviews were for all sorts of items. They tallied up the number of reviews that used past, present, and future tense, and then separately noted which reviews were marked as "helpful." They did also make some adjustments to control for extraneous variables such as the presence of photos, the length of the review, and the number of stars given by the reviewer (Maglio & Fung, 2024, "Time perspective and helpfulness: Are communicators more persuasive in the past, present, or future tense?" in *Journal of Experimental Social Psychology*).

Before reading on, see what you think:

"I was really pleased with how well this cable worked." (past)

"I'm going to get a lot of use out of this cable." (future)

"I love this cable. It's perfect." (present)

Which one seems more believable and trustworthy to you?

The researchers uncovered a pretty surprising pattern: the present tense reviews were significantly more likely to be marked as "helpful" by others than reviews that used past or future tense. Can you guess why?

Past tense language creates linguistic–and therefore emotional–distance. It sets events somewhere else in time and space, and that somehow makes those events feel less real, less important, and less relevant to the listener, and even to the speaker. On the other hand, present tense language creates a real-time experience in the moment, and this is something that can be shared and enjoyed by both people in the conversation, as though the event is unfolding right now. It's this shared sense of narrative participation that not only draws people closer to the story, but draws them closer to one another, as a collective audience for that story.

According to co-author Sam Maglio, "The more vivid something is, the more real and true it seems. The past and the future aren't as vivid as the present." He goes on to explain, "Reviews are maximally helpful when they are right here and they're right now, because the closer the reader can come to seeing it, touching it, making it palpable, the more they believe it and the more they trust it. It's hard to be immersive and vivid and visceral from a world away."

Look back to the dyslexic striper anecdotes above, and see how in the second story, it's as though you are right there with the speaker, first noticing the little dance, then the zipping up of the hoodie, all the way to the punch line, which is delivered in a way that makes you feel that you are hearing it for the first time, along with the speaker. They are not merely recounting something that is already finished and complete, but inviting you to participate in something that is actually unfolding right now–sounds way more fun, doesn't it?

A simple grammatical change can dramatically alter the listener's position relative to the story, and bring them in more closely. This ramps up feelings of engagement, investment, and intimacy, not just with the story itself but with the teller of the story. With this small change, you move from delivering a report, to painting a picture, then to inviting the other person to step into it.

How can we put Maglio and Fang's insights to use? The present tense can influence a lot more than just our everyday storytelling.

Notice tense in your own and others' language

First, simply become mindful of the way you usually recount stories. Granted, Maglio and Fang's research focused on Amazon reviews, but the principle likely applies to all kinds of communication. Challenge yourself to pay close attention and see what tense you most often speak in when engaging with others. You may be interested to note, also, what tense tended to accompany the more enjoyable or harmonious interactions, and what tense tended to go along with conversations you didn't enjoy as much.

Pay attention to the way people speak to you, or become curious about conversations you observe around you, even if that's just in movies or TV. When a dialogue seems to be flowing well, when there's chemistry or a story is told in a charming way, ask yourself what tense has been used to create that effect.

The more aware you become of the way that language influences engagement, the more you'll notice opportunities where you can make deliberate choices to create more immediacy. You might notice that in a slight disagreement, you're tempted to say, "I was annoyed when you forgot to mail that letter." Instead, you could say, "I'm feeling a little annoyed right now. I'm thinking of the thing with the letter this morning, and I'm just wanting to resolve it now."

This small shift to the present creates more intimacy and less distance. After all, if any problem solving is to occur, it will have to happen right there in the present.

Be curious and alive in the moment

Some conversations are "dead." The people having them are talking about something they're not really interested in, at arm's length. They may be repeating the same old things they always say, or parroting predictable phrases that they believe are required of them. In a very deep sense, talking in past tense is a way of deadening yourself to the life and spontaneity of the present moment–which is, after all, still happening, and not yet decided.

To let go of everything else and simply be alive to what is happening in the moment takes a degree of trust, a little vulnerability, and the willingness to play and explore. When you switch to present tense, this is not just a grammar change, but a change in perspective and in orientation. You're not just changing the words but changing the kind of conversation you are having. Consider the differences:

"I had such a good time with you last night."

"I'm having such a good time with you."

Or even:

"This is fun, isn't it?"

Be honest, direct, and present-focused

Immediacy almost always equals intimacy. Even if you're not telling a joke or anecdote, you can bring immense power and poignancy to what you say if you keep it focused on the real, living moment in front of you. All it takes is honestly and plainly acknowledging what is going on in the moment as it's going on, in real-time.

"Hearing you speak right now, you're reminding me of something…"

"I'm noticing a little spark of excitement here… Do you notice that, too?"

"Hm, I'm not sure about that. I'm trying to think of a response, but I'm drawing a blank."

"OK, this suddenly feels a little awkward, doesn't it?"

When you can radically arrive in the moment and have enough presence of mind to openly share and discuss what you find there, you may be surprised at just how much more real, connected, and fun your interactions become.

Key takeaways:

- In conversations, pauses (and the length of pauses) matter a lot. Pause too long and your message may be more cognitively difficult to process in the moment. Keep pauses at a quarter to half a second long, and a little longer after important or complex chunks of information to give people time to process. Be mindful of people's individual rhythms and synchronize with them where possible.
- Research shows that the speed at which people respond to one another in conversation is a great indictor of connection and rapport. By responding quickly (within 250 milliseconds), we can "click" with people and keep conversational energy high. Practice conversational pacing and encourage the other person to respond quickly, too.
- Research shows that social rewards activate the same parts of the brain associated with monetary reward. Compliments can be extremely effective in creating rapport, warmth, and trust,

but they have to be done well. The key is to be sincere, genuine, and specific, and to compliment something unique in them, in a way that is meaningful to the receiver.
- You can compliment appearance, skill, possessions, or personality. Compliments tend to follow a predictable formula. Try to compliment at the point where it's most relevant, and has the greatest chance of a positive impact. Always be aware of whether the compliment you'd like to pay is appropriate!
- Finally, use present tense when relating stories to create more intimacy, engagement, and presence. They're more entertaining, too!

Chapter 5: Navigating conflict, misunderstanding, and disagreement

It may be that "supercommunicators" are no better than anyone else when it comes to avoiding conflict and misunderstanding. What they *can* do, however, is navigate their way out again, after the inevitable tensions appear. Fear of conflict can make us less effective at managing it. To combat that, we can learn to shift our perspective and see the occasional conflict, misunderstanding, or disagreement as normal, manageable, and even productive aspects of communication.

When approached with a spirit of curiosity and a willingness to preserve connection, conflict can be appreciated as one quite powerful path to deeper, more authentic relationships.

Language is everything

When you think about it, language is magical. Sounds that you make with your lips and tongue can travel through the air, trigger a wave of electrochemical activity in another person's neural tissue, and ultimately trigger a cascade of associated images and understanding in their brains. Words, then, can literally *change minds*.

We've already seen how subtle things, like a pause a fraction of a second long, a quick reference to a shared memory, or a flash of perfectly timed eye contact can dramatically alter the path of conversation. The words we choose also have an enormous impact, and it's no exaggeration to say that a single word can make or break a dialogue. Consider the subtle difference between:

"OK, let me understand…"

"I'm trying to understand…"

"I don't understand."

"Help me understand…"

On a superficial level, each of these expressions is essentially conveying the same message. Dig a tiny bit deeper, however, and you'll see that there are vast oceans of nuance behind each one. One expresses frustration while another is more neutral; one emphasizes the trouble, while the other is focusing on the desire to *overcome* that trouble.

Elizabeth Stokoe is a British psychologist, communication expert, and professor of social interaction at Loughborough University. She has been studying the effect of language on human connection for years, and believes that even the tiniest differences in phrasing or word choice can have drastically different effects on people. In one research study, Stokoe uncovered the fact that patients tend to respond better when doctors present them with "options," for example, rather than speak at length about what is in their "best interests." The suggestions are the same in both cases–all that changes is the wording.

Words and phrases to use
"Would you be willing...?"

One of the words/phrases that Stokoe found particularly effective was "willing." She notes that in the middle of conflict, people tend to be more accommodating and cooperative when asked if they *would be willing* to do X or Y.

Something about this phrasing triggers people to answer in the affirmative, so it's a great way to frame requests when you sense the other person may be a little resistant. Perhaps these specific words activate a feeling of agency, dignity, and even generosity in the other person, rather than framing your request as something to resist or avoid.

Say something like, "I know it's not what we initially hoped for, but would you be willing to accept the work for this month and revisit the updated plan next month?"

Speak (not talk)

"We need to talk."

Sends a cold shiver down your spine, right? For whatever reason, the word "talk" has come to have heavy and mostly negative connotations for a lot of people.

Stokoe explains, "We observed this when looking at interactions between police negotiators and suicidal persons in crisis [...] negotiators who used phrases such as, 'I'm here to talk' were met with more resistance [...] Persons in crisis would often respond with something like: 'I don't want to talk, what's the point in talking?'"

If the word "speak" is used instead, this resistance seems to disappear, however. Culturally, "talk is cheap," and a person may be "all talk." Again, these associations may be completely unconscious, but they influence a person's receptiveness to your message all the same.

Say, "Can I speak to you about something?" or "Let's speak on Sunday about this."

Some (not any)

You're interacting with a professional of some kind and they say to you, "Is there anything else I can do for you today?"

It sounds fine, but actually, UCLA conversation experts John Heritage and Jeffrey Robinson wrote an entire chapter on it in the book *Applied Conversation Analysis* (2011, pg. 15-31, edited by Charles Antaki). They claim that in their investigations when doctors used "Is there *something* else I can do for you today?" with their patients, there was a better response than when they asked, "Is there *anything* else I can do for you today?"

The word "any" can feel too open-ended, too broad, and almost confrontational. It can put people on the spot. "Some" can feel smaller, more manageable, and more welcoming. Try to switch these out when you can. For example, instead of asking, "Do you have any questions?" you could say, "I've got time to answer some of your questions now."

Of course, if what you want to do is quickly put an end to the conversation and discourage questions, one of the best ways to do so is to briskly ask, "Any questions? No? OK, let's move on."

It seems like

Whether you're in a full-blown conflict or just trying to navigate your way out of a slightly awkward conversation, there's one important first step you can't miss: making sure the other person genuinely feels heard. According to Chris Voss, former FBI negotiator and author of the

2017 book *Never Split the Difference*, you cannot begin to influence another person unless you first take the time to listen to them.

If people feel unseen, unheard, and unacknowledged, they will continue to be defensive and resistant. The conversation will seem like a fight to them. Your first job is to make sure that you've truly heard their perspective and then demonstrate that fact to them. Paraphrase their position and make a show of confirming your comprehension:

"It seems like you're feeling XYZ right now, have I got that right?"

"Can I just check, do you mean that XYZ?"

You can paraphrase and confirm simply by repeating what they've said with minor tweaks. They may say, "I'm angry at you." and you can reflect back, "OK. I get that you're feeling angry, and I'm the one you're angry with."

Words and phrases to avoid

Just

"Can I just ask something?"

"I just wanted to say…"

"It's just an idea…"

This word just can be a way to hedge, or soften, the impact of what we're saying. Though of course it's necessary to be polite and tactful sometimes, overuse of this word can signal a lack of self-esteem, low confidence, or submissiveness. Sometimes, we really do want to ask for permission, to apologize, or to signal our shyness or submission; but when used in the wrong way, *just* can hurt our cause, creating an impression of self-negation.

There's no need to replace this word with anything, just try and eliminate it all together and see how your communication improves. Removing hedging language makes you come across as more secure and confident, and may also make you more likeable, since you'll be conveying a feeling of calmness and ease within yourself. Simply say what you want to say, without beating around the bush, or including little caveats, apologies, or bids for permission.

Other verbal tics and phrases to consider dropping:

- "Does that make sense?" (Especially when saying something perfectly sensible.)
- Um, like, you know (instead, just pause.)
- Prefacing everything you say with "I think," or "I feel," particularly if you're relaying objective facts.
- Maybe, could, might, possibly… (if you're sure about something, express that, rather than hedging.)

- Sorry (when you are not sorry or don't have anything to be sorry about!)

How are you today?

Now, Stokoe isn't saying to never ask this. But she does emphasize that this phrase can be annoying and invite resistance particularly when offered in a business or professional context. Think about how you'd feel if you called a customer help line and the representative began with, "And how are you today, sir?" What about if you were in a hurry to get through an embarrassing medical appointment and the nurse asked you this? Possibly, a little annoyed.

"Sales people are trained to do small talk at the beginning of calls, but we were able to show with our research that it doesn't work." says Stokoe. "Not only is there no evidence of reciprocal rapport-building, but also you're more likely to irritate the other person and extend the length of that call."

It's not the question itself that breaks rapport, but the suspicion that the sentiment behind it is fake. In work settings, Stokoe says you'll actually have more success just getting to the point, rather than pretending to care.

Yes, but...

"But" is a contrast word. Its entire function is to contrast what follows with what came before. When people hear "but," it's logical for them to assume that everything that came before is about to be cancelled out. That means that if you say something like, "I totally agree with what you're saying, but..." then it's more or less the same as saying, "I don't agree with what you're saying."

If the phrase "Yes, but" appears in your conversation, consider it a red flag that you may soon be involved in a tug-of-war, and not a conversation at all. It's not that disagreement itself or a difference of opinion is a threat; after all, many people find harmony and connection despite and even because of their differences. Rather, it's about making sure that you're not framing your contribution as something in opposition to theirs–i.e. as a threat.

Try to replace it with "Yes, and" So you can say, "Yes, I totally agree with what you're saying. And I also believe that XYZ..." Speak your piece without setting it in opposition to theirs. This is particularly effective if you've also taken the time to properly listen, reflect, and paraphrase, so they really do feel that you get their side: "It seems like you're worried about accuracy. And I'm most concerned about getting the pilot project done as quickly as possible..." By speaking in this way, you're opening up the psychological possibility of a joint solution with space for both accuracy *and* speed.

Magic words that smooth over conflict

Just as words like "but" can create and inspire conflict, there are others that do the opposite, smoothing over tension and friction. Those conversational geniuses among us will instinctively know which words these are and will be ready to quickly deploy them when conversations are starting to head south. For the rest of us, though, we may need to be a little more deliberate in our language choice–especially when conflict is beginning to rear its head.

Amanda Ripley is the author of *High Conflict: Why We Get Trapped and How We Get Out*, and she explains how **conflict is not really a problem at all–but the *frame* we place around conflict matters.** According to Ripley, there is such a thing as *productive conflict*–namely, there is always a way to engage with difference and disagreement without it threatening or undermining the connection between you and the other person.

All we need to do is learn to create dialogue that's about cooperation. Yet again we find ourselves back at the mindset game: When we see difficult conversations as opportunities for learning, new understanding, depth, and the creation of intimacy and trust, then conflict is manageable. On the other hand, when we frame this difficulty as a threat to us personally, as something scary to avoid, as a bad sign that something is wrong, or, worst of all, as a problem caused by the other person, then we are on the fast track to yet more conflict.

The shift that Ripley talks about all through her book is a mental one, and it's none other than the change in mindset we've investigated in this book, too. We can demonstrate a cooperative mindset as well as encourage it in others by our choice of language. With our language we can convey so much, most importantly that no matter what, we are interested in connection more than we are interested in winning or being right.

Here are some phrases that capture the cooperative spirit Ripley is talking about:

- "I wonder if..."
- "We definitely agree on that."
- "It's interesting that you say that, because I see it differently..."
- "I might be wrong about this, but..."
- "How funny! I had a different reaction..."
- "I'm curious. How did you arrive at that conclusion?"
- "Can you tell me more about why you think so?"
- "I'm seeing things a little differently."

- "I'm a little nervous about saying this, but..."
- "I'm not sure about that, can you help me understand?"
- "I hope we can solve this together."
- "On the one hand, I see what you're saying. On the other hand..."
- "Have I understood you correctly?"
- "I never thought about it that way. Can you walk me through it?"
- "Maybe I've misunderstood."
- "From my perspective... What about yours?"

It's not that these specific phrases hold any power or magic–rather, it's the spirit and intention behind them. They all express a desire to cooperate, connect, understand, and problem solve. Notice the use of "we" (psychologically putting you together, rather than at odds) and the use of questions to continually invite input.

You want to avoid defensiveness in yourself as well as avoid triggering it in others. Why would people be defensive? Because they perceive something as worth defending against, i.e. they perceive a threat. This means that the main goal of conflict-defusing communication is to dial down any feelings of threat or fear, and dial up feelings of teamwork, trust, and mutual solution-finding. In couple's therapy, this is sometimes expressed as: "It's you and me vs. the problem; never you vs. me."

Convert conflict into cooperation

Let's be honest–in the heat of an emotional conversation, you might not easily remember this or that phrase. Especially if you're feeling misunderstood, unheard, insulted, or threatened, your instinct may be to go on the defensive, or to more forcefully make your own claim. But that would be a mistake. During difficult conversations, our main goal should be to maintain presence of mind. We should consistently try to sustain and elicit an attitude of willingness, openness, and compassion. Easier said than done, of course!

Nevertheless, there are a few "magic words" that can snap us out of the conflict mindset and back into a healthier perspective.

Turn disagreement into curiosity

Flat-out disagreement is a wall. It terminates understanding and ends dialogue. Instead, frame the situation as a curiosity. Say, "That's so interesting..." and simply offer an observation. The attitude is one of, "We seem to be in different places on this, isn't that fascinating?"

If you can approach problems not as problems at all, but rather as unthreatening phenomena, then you are better primed to engage with them, rather than to instantly go to war.

"No, you said you wanted it for Friday, not Thursday. That's what you said."

"Oh, really? That's so interesting. I could have sworn I sent you an email asking for Thursday. What shall we do now?"

"Well, I can't get it done by Thursday, I'm afraid. But I'll do my best. Is late Thursday afternoon OK?"

"That would really be helpful, thank you."

As you can see, the entire approach has nothing to do with who's right, who's to blame, or what "really happened." All that matters is solving the problem at hand with calm curiosity while maintaining harmony and connection. In a 2017 paper by Fisher et. al. ("The Influence of Social Interaction on Intuitions of Objectivity and Subjectivity" in *Cognitive Science*), the authors explain that,

> "Participants who engaged in cooperative interactions were less inclined to agree that there was an objective truth about that topic than were those who engaged in a competitive interaction [...] When people are in cooperative arguments, they see the truth as more subjective."

Turn the absolute into the personal

For the same reason, absolute blanket statements can act like death knells for conversations. Instead, keep things specific and human-scale. Instead of saying, "This is an outrage!" you can say, "This situation has made me quite upset."

Not only is the latter less likely to arouse resistance, it's also more accurate. Think of it this way: Nobody can engage with an absolute, but it's always possible to work with the human being in front of you, and the specific issue they're dealing with at this particular moment.

Turn judgment and condemnation into sharing experience

"You're being disrespectful." and "I don't feel respected." are a universe apart, even though their literal meaning is arguably the same. If you preface your observations and thoughts with "I feel," or "I think," or "From my point of view," you are transforming the conversation from a fact-finding mission into one where people are merely sharing their experiences and perspectives.

This is not a replacement for "the truth," nor is it a way to arrive at it; rather, it's a switch in perspective that creates the possibility of empathy. After all, many conflicts and disagreements do not take place in the objective realm of fact, but rather in that wishy washy, gray area of our own personal experiences and interpretations. Respecting and understanding how we differ *here* is the start of real compassion and understanding.

Certainty, stubbornness, judgment, and the ego's insistence on being right are all things that kill a conversation, and drain away rapport and connection. Curiosity, on the other hand, keeps things alive.

E-prime language

Consider an argument people might have:

"This TV show is stupid."

"No it's not. It's actually really clever."

"Nah, it's stupid."

What makes a conversation like this such a stalemate? According to the theory behind *E-prime language*, it's the presence of "to be" verbs, which all imply a fixed, objective, and unchanging reality. When the person says the TV show **is** or **isn't** stupid, their language is actually muddled. That's because he is presenting his opinion as a fact. He is actually inviting disagreement, namely with the person who wants to say the show **is** something else. Indeed, if someone says, "*I personally find* this show stupid." there is not much to argue with, right?

"You are being unfair."

"I'm not happy."

"There's only one way out of this."

All of these are just assumptions, feelings, interpretations, and expectations masquerading as permanent facts. It's a strange feature of human language: I can say, for example, "It is my fault." and I may be convinced that this is now a true fact about reality simply because the grammatical structure so strongly suggests it. This language can not only dramatically influence how we see ourselves, but it can also radically shape the way we encounter one another in dialogue.

The idea is that this kind of language keeps us stuck and prevents us from properly connecting to one another. When you say something like, "You *are* a difficult person." it is a claim about reality that has definite consequences for the way you think and perceive. When directed towards someone else, it will definitely impact them! According to E-prime, the only way to get things moving again is to be mindful of and carefully avoid "to be" verbs like is, am, was, are, etc.

The theory was first introduced in 1933 by Alfred Korzybski, and is fundamentally about how our language shapes our perception. **By shifting our language, we shift our perception, opening ourselves to more**

dynamic and adaptable conversations with others.

This is a profound challenge: When we speak, we need to pay attention to what we're actually saying. If we say, "This is impossible." is it *really* true? Is that reality we're talking about, or are we just making a value judgment or sharing our emotion? If we unquestioningly make a pronouncement about what is and isn't possible, then what more is there to think about or converse about? It is far more accurate to say, "I'm having difficulty with this." *That* opens the door to conversation-and problem solving.

The E-prime concept is complex and deserves more attention than we can give it in these pages, but here are some insights it can offer when it comes to better, more harmonious conversations:

- **Eliminate "to be" verbs** where possible, or at least abandon the spirit of speaking as though one possesses absolute knowledge of objective truth. A simple example: Instead of saying, "It's hot in here." you can say "I feel hot." Your language instantly becomes more truthful, less conflictual, and clearer.
- **Let go of the need to be right**, and don't be afraid of changing your mind, admitting mistakes, or being uncertain. Human beings are actually certain of a lot less than they'd like to admit.

Conversation implies process, and that implies imperfection, change, and uncertainty. Embrace that. Rather than, "I don't like this." say, "I'm not sure how I feel about this at the moment."

- **If you must label, label experiences, emotions, and situations, *not* people.** Never say, "You are X." to someone. Nobody is ever defined by a single idea, thought, feeling, or event. Instead of, "You're wrong." say, "I'm not sure I agree with you on that." Instead of, "You're confused." say, "Help me understand what you mean by that."
- **Be careful with your language.** "Michael Jackson was the single greatest recording artist in the history of the world." is not clean language. "I love Michael Jackson." is far more accurate.

Science-backed ways to end (or escape) a conversation

If you're diligently practicing your active listening skills, asking thoughtful follow-up questions, and being playful and curious as you contribute your best to the conversation, you may discover something interesting. You could be the best conversationalist in the world and still want it all to end. Can you relate?

Perhaps you've found yourself stuck in a tedious dialogue that you can't seem to claw your way out of. It's all well and good knowing how to introduce yourself, tell a good story and chat comfortably with the other person, but then what? If you've ever felt like you're slowly dying as the other person goes on and on and on... You're not alone.

No, really, you aren't. Consider this: The other person who seemingly won't let you go *feels exactly the same as you do.*

The feeling that we are the only ones who wish a conversation would end may simply be a bias or illusion. That's the finding of a paper by researcher Mastroianni and colleagues, titled "Do Conversations End When People Want Them To?"

Long story short, the answer to the question in the title is *no*. The authors conclude that conversations rarely end when people actually want them to. In one experiment, participants were paired with a stranger and asked to speak anywhere from 1 to 45 minutes. They were later asked to report back a) when they wanted the conversation to stop and b) when they guessed the other person wanted the conversation to stop.

Findings were surprising. The conversations basically never ended when people wanted them to, and there was an enormous discrepancy between what people wanted and how long the talk actually lasted. The researchers found that not only were people bad at guessing when others wanted to stop talking (that is, they often assumed they wanted to continue when they didn't) they also weren't good at noticing when they themselves were losing interest.

What this means is that feeling trapped in conversations is not uncommon... and it also means that while you're feeling trapped and trying to find a way to escape politely, the other person may be in precisely the same predicament!

Mastroianni and colleagues called the whole thing a "coordination problem." Out of politeness, people may conceal all those little signals that may reveal our genuine desire to stop talking, but if both people are doing the same thing, you can easily see why conversations keep going when nobody is enjoying them. "Even though conversations are one big coordination failure," Mastroianni says philosophically, "they're really fun." He explains, "All of this coordination failure may be in service of relationship success [...] People enjoy them more than they think they will. So rather than scheming and strategizing about how to get out of them, maybe just sit back and enjoy them."

Knowing that people are bad at estimating the right length for a conversation, bad at estimating their own preferences for length, and *really* bad at noticing when someone else is wanting to stop, what on earth can we do? One option is to strategically end conversations sooner than you think is actually polite. In other words, it's preferable to leave people wanting more, than to overstay your conversational welcome.

Also, realize that conversations don't end sooner simply because people don't know that others want them to. In other words, our politeness is getting in the way. You can help by politely and clearly signaling when you're ready to end and being ready to notice the same in others. Granted, the latter may be harder than the former.

A few ways to navigate all this:

- Be clear upfront about how long you expect conversation to last. "Oh, hi Lydia! So nice to see you. I have to be in town in 10 minutes' time, but I'd love to chat for a moment. Tell me, how did that thing with your mother-in-law go?" Not only does this give the other person something to work with, but it gives you something to refer back to when you're ready to wrap up.
- Another way to achieve the same effect is to attach your conversations to an activity with a clear and fixed time limit. If you plan to have coffee, walk the dog, or share a train ride together, it's quite clear when each of these activities are over. In professional contexts this is even easier, as you can be quite transparent in how

long you have scheduled for each conversation.
- Be very obvious in communicating your satisfaction with the conversation that's just passed, even though you're ending it. Express that you've enjoyed talking, and make the other person feel appreciated and valued. Phrases like "It's been such a treat to catch up." or "I always enjoy chatting with you." act as the necessary reassurance that the conversation is ending on happy terms.
- Though politeness tends to forbid saying outright, "I'm ready to stop talking to you now" there are plenty of nonverbal ways to gracefully signal your readiness to move on. Standing up when you've been sitting, clearing your throat, arranging your things, putting on coats or hat, or subtly moving towards the exit are all good ways to neatly wrap up a conversation.
- Verbal ways to end the conversation include summarizing language. Pointedly stop adding any new information and instead use wrapping up language, or begin to talk about the conversation itself in the past tense. "I'm glad you told me that story, that was amazing. We should do this again sometime." This implies that we have already "done" this, and now it's finished!

- "Closing rituals" and phrases like, "So anyway," or "Right, so…," may reliably indicate a scene change, as can a sigh or a gesture like clapping the hands together or patting the lap.
- Finally, a good trick is to make plans for when to meet again. For most people, this will not only signal the conversation's end, but will also reassure them that it has been a successful conversation, so they can happily bid you adieu.

Mastroianni seems to suggest that the coordination problem he discovered was simply a fact of life and an endearing human quirk. Knowing that we all struggle a little socially, even though we hide it, can actually create a surprising sense of compassion and forgiveness for both ourselves and others. The next time you're in a boring conversation, remember his research and be bold–bowing out gracefully may feel risky, but you just might bring an enormous sense of relief to the other person!

Dealing with conversational narcissists

We'll end our book on a topic that may have already been on your mind for some time now: What do you do when you're trapped with someone who genuinely just wants to talk and talk and talk and talk?

Though most of us are doing our best, it's true to say that there are indeed self-absorbed and socially unaware people you'll likely engage with. There will always be someone ready and willing to take full advantage of all these great listening skills you're trying to develop. They may seem utterly uninterested in your perspective, rude, demanding, and lacking in tact and empathy. What then?

If you're feeling talked over, held hostage, or otherwise mistreated in a conversation, relax: it's not pleasant, but it *is* normal, and it's not the end of the world. There are a few ways out:

First, give the other person the benefit of the doubt. We all have our bad days, and we can all occasionally find ourselves in less-than-ideal moods. Cut people some slack. Let them talk, try to show an interest in where they're coming from, and do your best to signal a genuine curiosity in them. Some people may (understandably) be wrestling with a very real need to feel heard and seen, and may seldom get the opportunity to feel like someone is actually listening to them. You could be the person to offer them that opportunity.

That said, none of us are required to offer endless conversational charity and be impromptu therapists and sounding boards for people who have no intention of returning the favor. If you find that a person consistently flouts the give-and-take rules of conversation, try not to feel any guilt about putting down firm boundaries.

You can be polite, kind, and perfectly reasonable even as you protect your time and energy. Conversational narcissism is a growing problem in our modern world, but you can set clear limits for yourself. Try not to take offense, keep it light, and bring a little humor into things. Remind yourself that you never have to suffer for someone else's benefit, and that relationships of all kinds need to be mutually fulfilling to be sustainable over time. The more you develop your own conversational skills, the more aware you will be of other peoples' skill–or lack thereof. Try to be patient, but give yourself permission to walk away from conversations that aren't going anywhere!

Key takeaways:

- Language matters, and a single word can make or break a conversation. Use "would you be willing," "speak," (not talk) and "some" (not any). Avoid words that signal disagreement like "yes, but" and "just," which can minimize and undermine what you're saying.
- Conflict is not a problem and not something to be afraid of. However, the frame we place around conflict makes all the difference, and often this comes down to language. Deliberately use phrases and expressions that smooth over tension and emphasize collaboration.

- "Productive conflict" means engaging with difference and disagreement without allowing it to threaten or undermine rapport. Turn disagreement into curiosity (by asking questions), turn the absolute into the personal, and turn judgment and condemnation into a chance to share your own experience.
- Using E-prime language, we become more mindful of and avoid "to be" verbs in conversation, and aim to speak more clearly, distinguishing fact from opinion. Pay attention to what you're actually saying. Be careful with language, let go of the need to be right or certain when you aren't, and if you must label, label experiences, emotions, and situations, *not* people.
- The feeling that we are the only ones who wish a conversation would end may simply be a bias or illusion. We are bad at judging when others want to end conversations, but most people tend to want to end sooner than others would guess. Don't be afraid to cut things short and leave them wanting more.
- Finally, be patient with people who are not as attentive or empathetic as you like, but for *persistent* conversational narcissists, give yourself permission to set up boundaries to protect your time and energy.

Bonus Chapter: Conversation prompts

When it comes to brushing up on your communication skills, **practice makes perfect.** Because it's so important to consistently put what you learn into practice through deliberate action, I've included this bonus section of fun games and prompts to help you flex your developing conversation muscles.

There are 52 in all, each one a little different. These are games, yes, but they're also pretty powerful ways to practice connecting with others in the moment, to think on your feet, to navigate sudden conversational twists and turns, and to gracefully maneuver through tension and awkwardness. Each exercise will make you more socially limber, articulate, relaxed, and confident.

By their nature, these exercises cannot be done alone, so find someone else who's willing to work on their communication skills too, and set aside some time to have fun with it. Think of these games as a kind of practice arena, and a place where you can experiment and learn before bringing those abilities into the real world. Do a few at a time, or challenge yourself to try one a day–it's up to you!

When you're done, take a moment to reflect. How did you find the game? What did you learn? I know it can feel a little awkward and even intimidating at first, but I guarantee that if you lean into those exercises that seem the trickiest, you'll turbo-charge your progress–and along with it, your social confidence. Find someone who is also interested in brushing up on their conversational skills, and, if you like, ask them for feedback. You may be surprised by just how much, and just how fast, you learn.

1. **You'Alphabet Game** - In this activity, each person takes turns saying something related to a topic, starting with the following letter of the alphabet.

For example:

Player 1: Apple pie is my favorite dessert.

Player 2: Bananas are a close second.

The first person chooses a topic, like favorite foods, games, movies, etc. Do this until all twenty-six letters in the alphabet have been used, proving once and for all that you've mastered the ABCs of wit and wisdom!

2. **Excuses Game** - Accuse the person next to you using questions like "Why are you late?" or "Why didn't you take the garbage out?" The accused player quickly comes up with a creative and funny excuse. Rotate to the next player after each round, and the previously accused player becomes the accuser.

Continue until everyone has taken a turn as an accuser, keeping excuses extraordinary and entertaining without going overboard.

3. **Childhood Blunders** - Choose an embarrassing tale from your childhood. Share the story for only **two** minutes. Narrate it in the third-person perspective. No one judges here, so aim to keep your account within the time limit while adding humor and detail to engage the listeners.

4.   **Movie Detective** - Ask the person next to you about a movie, book, or other media they recently read and enjoyed. Once they share, ask one open-ended question to explore why they liked it. Then, become the detective and try to understand their thoughts about the movie- what they didn't like, the characters, the plot, the cinematography, etc.

Keep the conversation going until you've asked **five** questions. Sharpen your question-asking skills, uncovering the nuances of their experience with each inquiry.

5.   **Conversational Quest** - Let the laughter roll in as you dive into a dialogue using only questions! If someone asks, "What is the weather like on Mars?" fire back with a playful, "Where did I leave my space umbrella?" But here's the catch-in large groups, answer with a statement, and you're out!

Keep the fun going for up to three rounds in small groups. Ready, set, question time-let the good vibes flow!

6. **Setting Boundaries with Grace** - Role-play a scenario where you ask your conversation partner to invite you to a wedding and then simulate declining with a kind response that asserts your boundary. You really want to go, but...

Take turns and continue the role-play until each participant has successfully set their boundary in three different ways.

7. **Terrible Gifts** - Think of the most terrible present you've ever received and get ready to turn it into a convincing gem! Your mission: Persuade the person next to you that this dreaded gift is surprisingly helpful for one minute.

Keep playing until each player successfully transforms their terrible gift and convinces their neighbor of its usefulness.

8. **Weather Banter** - Come up with three fun ways to answer, "How's the weather?" First, give a regular weather update. Then, make the next two replies funny and interesting to keep the conversation lively. Share all three answers, and the banter concludes, turning a basic weather chat into a delightful exchange. Play until everyone shares their three responses, creating a sunny atmosphere even on the cloudiest of days!

9. **Exaggerated Mishaps** - Share a recent work mishap and exaggerate its impact on your life or the world. For example, if discussing a minor inconvenience, claim that it caused a global crisis. This is how you make your life sound like a series of stories.

Continue the storytelling fun until each participant has shared their exaggerated mishap.

10. **Banter Extravaganza** - Kick off the fun with a simple fact about yourself, like "I like chocolate," and brace yourself for laughs as the next person playfully exaggerates, saying

something like, "You're so sweet that ants want to be friends with you."

Keep the banter rolling, making it over the top each time. The game ends if someone fails to comment for three seconds. Get ready for a good time and lots of laughs, but beware of the three-second silence—it might just end the banter extravaganza!

11. **Pop Culture Descriptors** - Pick a pop culture reference like "Game of Thrones" and swap out ordinary adjectives to vividly describe your favorite food. Picture saying, "I love pizza because it's 'Game of Thrones' addictive-it rules my taste buds with a kingdom of flavors!" Keep the fun rolling until everyone has shared their pop culture-infused descriptions. Have fun weaving pop culture into your daily chatter!

12. **The Good, The Nice, and The Ugly** - Share two glowing positives about something you cherish or are passionate about. For instance, "I adore my morning coffee; it's an energizing ritual and has a perfect blend of flavors."

For the third element, take a humorous turn and share a negative aspect. Picture this: "Yet, the beverage has me questioning my life choices—like facing a surprise quiz in adulthood." Keep playing until everyone has shared their trio of insights—two positives and one amusingly negative twist.

13.   **Occupational Comedy** - Share your occupation with your conversation partner or group. Instead of a typical response like "I'm a marketing executive," vividly describe the humorous drama you encounter in your job. Make the menial sound enormous. Engage your listener by weaving a tale that captures the essence of your daily work adventures for one minute. It's not just about what you do, but how you share it.

Continue the occupational comedy storytelling until each participant has had their one-minute spotlight.

14.   **Save the Cat Adventure** - Think about a memorable adventure you had recently. Share

your story using a "Save The Cat" structure. Your tale ends ensuring you cover all 15 beats. Use the questions below as your guide when you tell your story:

1. Opening Image: What was the very first moment that started your adventure?

2. Theme Stated: What's the main thing you learned during your journey?

3. Set-Up: Who are you, and what was your life like before the adventure?

4. Catalyst: What unexpected event kicked off your adventure?

5. Debate: What were you thinking as you decided whether to go on the adventure or not?

6. Break into Two: What specific choice did you make to start your journey?

7. B Story: Did someone else play a big role in your adventure? How?

8. Fun and Games: What were the main challenges you faced, and what did you learn from them?

9. Midpoint: What moment changed the course of your adventure?

10. Bad Guys Close In: How did things get more challenging?

11. All Is Lost: When was the lowest point of your journey?

12. Dark Night of the Soul: What made you stop and think about your journey?

13. Break into Three: How did you get ready for the final part of your adventure?

14. Finale: What happened at the end when you faced the biggest challenges?

15. Final Image: What's the last thing you remember, like a snapshot of your journey?

15. **Silent Storm Report** - Pretend you're a weatherman, but no talking allowed! Show the approaching storm using only your body language—big gestures and expressive faces. Make the intensity and impact crystal clear without saying a word. Continue this fun challenge until you've reached one minute. It's a delightful exercise that sharpens your nonverbal skills, adding drama to your forecast.

16. **Polite Product Declines** - Choose a conversation partner and take turns playing roles. One will be a persistent salesman, and the other just needs to come up with three responses that are polite yet assertive. Sharpen your ability to gracefully decline while maintaining a positive tone and preserving the relationship.

Continue the role-playing exercise until each participant has taken a turn as both the salesman and the one declining the product. The game concludes once everyone has practiced coming up with three polite yet assertive responses, turning the interaction into a constructive exercise in communication skills.

17. **Imaginary Company Tale** - Choose a random word that starts with the letter B from a dictionary. Think of five related words and select two randomly. Create an imaginary company name with those two words and craft a creative story about this fictional company in one minute. Strengthen your storytelling skills by weaving an imaginative narrative that brings your made-up company to life.

After your turn, the other participants should share their imaginary company name using another letter. The game ends when everyone has completed their turn, resulting in a collection of diverse and vivid tales about various fictional businesses.

18. **Connecting the Unlikely** - Get creative by finding three surprising ways to link the world's worst superhero with a time-traveling device. Think outside the box and make up a fun story that brings these two topics together in unexpected ways. It's all about having fun and letting your imagination run wild!

Take turns with your conversation partner until each person has shared three surprising connections between the world's worst superhero and a time-traveling device.

19. **Pitch Play: Nursery Edition** - Recite a nursery rhyme as if it were a story, using contrasting tones. Begin with a dull monotone, then switch to a lively, vibrant rendition—experimenting with pitch, tone, and pacing. Be over the top, with each emotion being expressed in a ridiculous way. Stretch your emotional

range. This is how you are more easily understood.

After your turn, each participant will do the same thing with a different nursery rhyme. Keep going until every participant has showcased their creative interpretations.

20. **Meet the Scientist** - If you could meet any famous scientist, who would it be? Think of five W questions (who, what, when, where, and why) you would ask them. It's a fun exercise to enhance your questioning skills—craft inquiries that dig into their work and motivations. Dive into this imaginary interview and sharpen your curiosity.

After your turn, the other participants will do the same thing with a different scientist of their choice. Keep it up until everyone has shared the five questions they would ask during their imaginary interviews.

21. **Collective Memory Lane** - Kick things off with a pretend memory, like "Do you remember when we sailed paper boats in a

puddle?" Each person chips in their own twist, such as "Yeah, but then it rained... with dancing water droplets!"

Keep it light and fun with surprises, go around until everyone adds their twist or for two rounds. Enjoy the laughs and creative journey together!

22. **Bizarre Food Encounter** - Each person has one minute to share a story about the strangest food they've ever eaten and their exaggerated reactions. Use facial expressions and gestures like a stand-up comedian to turn that weird experience into a source of laughs.

The game ends once everyone has had their one-minute turn, leaving the room filled with laughter and amusing food tales.

23. **Unusual Hobby Challenge** - Pair up with someone and ask them to suggest a hobby you'd typically dismiss, such as extreme ironing. Instead of saying "no," respond with a "yes...and." Drop your thoughts, embrace the idea, and inject playfulness into the conversation. Challenge

yourself to turn the mundane into something uniquely enjoyable–like transforming the ironing board into a surfboard or adding a touch of dance. Share your "yes...and" twist to make this unconventional hobby proposal exciting!

After your turn, switch roles with your partner. The activity ends once both participants have shared their "yes...and" twists, fostering a playful atmosphere of creative exploration.

24. **Non-Verbal Emotion Challenge** - Use facial expressions and body language to convey strong emotions (like anger) without words. See if others can guess the feeling you're portraying. Mastering the art of silent drama is the first step to becoming the Meryl Streep of social interactions.

After your turn, the other participants will take their chance to convey the specified emotions with a different twist–perhaps adding a touch of humor or drama. The game ends after everyone has showcased their non-verbal acting skills, turning silent expressions into a guessing game filled with emotions and entertainment.

25. **The Witty Palm Reader** - Let the palmistry adventure begin! Take the hand of the person to your right, squint at it with a twinkle in your eye, and come up with three hilariously specific predictions for their personal life, career, and love life. For example, "I predict you'll become a sock-finding champion in your personal life, a multitasking superhero in your career, and experience a love life as sweet and surprising as discovering hidden chocolate in your pantry!"

Continue the laughter-filled fortune-telling fiesta until everyone has had a chance to become a palm reader.

26. **Assumption Adventure** - Start the game by creating a leading statement, making an assumption about your conversation partner, and saying it out loud. It could be as simple as "You must love hiking." or "I bet you're a crossword puzzle pro." Their task is to either confirm or deny your assumption and share the story behind it. See how leading statements, instead of direct questions, can bring flow to ordinary discussions.

After your turn, switch roles, and the person next to you makes an assumption about you. Continue this assumption adventure until everyone has had a chance to play both roles.

27. **Witty Object Affiliation** - Each person in the group randomly selects an object in the room. By creatively associating yourself with your chosen object, channel your inner wit and humor. For example, "I'm like this pail because I handle all the leaks in this room!"

Do this until each participant has shared their playful connection.

28. **Frustration Validation** - Describe a frustrating scenario from your own life. Each person from the group should give validation without offering solutions or advice. See if you can turn this frustrating moment into a riveting tale because who doesn't love a good story about triumphing over life's little annoyances? Practice your validating statements.

After your turn, each participant takes a moment to share their own frustrating scenario, and the rest of the group provides validation without offering solutions. Continue this frustration validation exercise until everyone has had a chance to share their stories and receive empathetic validation.

29. **Misunderstanding and Solutions** - Share a funny story about a misunderstanding you had with someone, and then discuss how it could have been avoided with clear communication. After all, navigating the maze of miscommunication is an art—master it, and you'll be the Picasso of conversation.

After your turn, each participant shares their own amusing tale of misunderstanding and discusses potential solutions through clear communication. Continue this exploration of miscommunication and solutions until everyone has had a chance to contribute.

30. **The unconventional Pen Pitch** - Time for the 'Sell a Pen' challenge! Picture yourself as a charismatic salesperson. Your job is to convince the group to buy this amazing pen.

Share why it's a game-changer using your experience, tell a personal story, use colorful language, and sprinkle in some interesting data.

Keep going until one person is convinced to buy the pen. Let's show that selling a pen is all about a good story, charm, and a bit of statistical magic. Let the pen-selling fun begin!

31. **Quirky Tale Twist** - Share a snippet of a funny or embarrassing moment. Your story will be considered a 'donkey.' Now, invite your conversation partner to add a quirky 'tail'—a delightful addition that showcases their humor and support. For example, if you say, "I unintentionally spilled coffee on my office desk," your partner might add a 'tail' like, "Did your colleagues start calling it the Java Jungle exhibit?" Elevate the humor and camaraderie in your conversation.

After your turn, your partner will be the one to share their story, and you will add a 'tail.' The exchange ends when both have shared their donkey story and received a creative 'tail' twist.

32. **Outsmarting the Bully** - Pair up with someone, and they will take the bully role, throwing some teasing your way. For instance, they might say, "Nice shirt. Did you get it from the grandma section?" Now, in this role-play, respond with a witty comeback like "Yep, and it came with a side of grandma's secret weapon– her legendary cookie recipe." Sharpen your ability to handle teasing with humor and confidence.

Afterward, switch roles, and it's your partner's chance to respond to your teasing. Continue the role-play until each participant has had a chance to be the one outsmarting the bully.

33. **Word Wonders Comedy Jam** - Each participant contributes just one word to a story, but here's the twist: make it surreal and unexpected. Build on the quirky contributions of others to create a comedic masterpiece that'll have everyone in stitches. The goal? To collectively craft a hilarious tale that defies logic and keeps the laughs rolling in! So, one word at a time, let the whimsical wordplay fiesta begin!

For large groups, continue this whimsical wordplay fiesta until everyone has contributed.

For small groups of 2-5, keep it going for three rounds.

34. **Upside-Downside** - Kick off the conversation by making a statement starting with "upside". For instance, "Upside, I discovered a secret treasure map." The person next to you carries on the adventure by introducing a "downside" statement like "Downside, the map was written in an ancient language I couldn't decipher."

Keep the momentum going as the next person responds with another upside, and the pattern continues. Do this until each player has contributed both their upsides and downsides or for three rounds. Embrace the unexpected narrative twists and turns, savoring the laughter that naturally unfolds!

35. **Word Link Game** - The cardholder must start by saying a random sentence. For instance, Player 1 says, "The sun sets over the mountains." The next person then starts the following sentence using the **last** word of the previous player. Player 2 responds with, "Mountains

provide breathtaking views." Player 3 continues, "Views like these inspire inner peace."

Players who can't make their sentences correctly are disqualified and taken out of the game. Continue this linguistic relay until a final winner emerges, showcasing a skillful connection of sentences.

36. **Mirthful Motivation** - Imagine being a motivational speaker at a conference for people having a bad day. Craft a funny and uplifting speech that turns their frowns upside down. Include unexpected motivational tips and quirky anecdotes to bring laughter to the room.

Keep the mirthful motivation flowing until you hit the two-minute mark.

37. **Sarcastic Advice Column** - Play the role of an advice columnist, and each participant should seek your advice. Respond to imaginary problems or real-life dilemmas with a dose of sarcasm. For example, someone might ask, "How do I deal with stress at work?" You can reply

with, "Oh, just take up juggling chainsaws during your coffee breaks. It's a proven stress-buster."

Do this until everyone has received their advice. Turn the advice column into a lighthearted and humorous exchange.

38. **Conversational Pairing** - Start with a noun, like "mountain," and the person beside you must add a verb, such as "hiking," forming the creative pair "mountain hiking."

Now, the next person must connect the formed pair with a creative explanation, for example, "A mountain hikes by growing lush trails with invisible footsteps." (This is intentionally vague and nonsensical.) Keep the chat flowing until everyone has contributed their imaginative connections or for three rounds, making conversations more exciting and fun!

39. **Musical Discovery Adventure** - Begin the conversation by inquiring about a musical artist that resonates with your partner. Respond with EDR. Express the emotions you perceive based on their answer (Emotion). Then,

immerse yourself in the details by asking thoughtful W questions, uncovering the nuances of their feelings about the chosen artist and the joy of sharing musical preferences (Detail). Lastly, summarize their insights, echoing them back for confirmation to strengthen understanding (Restatement).

Switch roles; now it's your partner's turn to lead the exchange. The conversation ends after both participants have completed their EDR response.

40. **Redirection Challenge** - Picture this: someone asks about quantum physics, a topic not in your wheelhouse. Respond with a clever redirection, like, "While I'm not a quantum expert, I know a lot about... underwater basket weaving." Turn those moments of uncertainty into witty redirections and keep the banter flowing with unexpected twists.

Continue the redirection challenge until everyone has showcased their ability to turn moments of uncertainty into witty and unexpected banter.

41.   **Story Retelling** - Pair up with person on your right and share a personal story about how you conquered a fear. Your partner must restate the story, focusing on emotional expressions and details, deepening the connection. Then, switch roles, and the exchange ends after your conversation partner is done sharing their story and when you're done retelling it. Transform anecdotes into a shared experience that forges stronger connections.

42.   **Entrepreneurial Dreams Dialogue** - Initiate the conversation by prompting your partner to share a business idea they dream of pursuing. Respond with HPM. First, tell them what their experience reminds you of (History). Then, reflect on your take on business in general (Philosophy). Lastly, use a metaphor to represent the other person's entrepreneurial dream (Metaphor). Switch roles, and the exchange ends after your conversation partner shares their business dream and when you're done completing the HPM. Enhance the conversation by blending personal stories, beliefs, and symbols for a deeper exploration of shared entrepreneurial visions.

43. **Job Jubilation** - Ask your conversation partner about a recent work win. Then, respond using SBR. First, ask about the highlights, funny moments, or quirky things that made it a memorable experience (Specific). Then, dive into the journey—whether it felt like a rollercoaster, a smooth ride, or a comedy of errors (Broad). Wrap it up with a touch of humor by sharing a lighthearted work-related tale or an amusing anecdote (Related). Switch roles, and the exchange ends after your conversation partner shares their recent work win and when you're done with your SBR response. Amp up the fun with a mix of specific and broad questions for an entertaining and relaxed exchange!

44. **Vacation Swap** - Ask your conversation partner about their recent vacation. Then, respond using SBR. Start with inquiring about the highlights, unexpected moments, and things that made it special (Specific). Then, ask how they got there. Was it a road trip, a flight, or something else (Broad)? Lastly, share your own experience related to their travel story (Related). Switch roles, and the exchange ends after your conversation partner shares their recent work win and when you're done with

your SBR response. Level up your interaction by incorporating specific and broad questions, along with related statements, for a more engaging and meaningful exchange.

45. **Overcoming Challenges** - Ask your conversation partner how they overcame a significant challenge. Respond again with HPM. First, reply with what their experience reminds you of (History). Then, share your take on resilience and personal growth (Philosophy). Lastly, use a metaphor to represent the other person's path to success (Metaphor). Switch roles, and the exchange ends after your conversation partner shares their business dream and when you're done completing the HPM. Elevate the dialogue by intertwining personal narratives, beliefs, and symbolic insights.

46. **Openness Exploration** - Ask your conversation partner about their honest thoughts on playing the conversation game. Use EDR when replying. First, respond with the emotions you perceive based on their answer. (Emotion) Then, dive into the details by asking W questions to understand their feelings about participating in the game. (Detail) Lastly, summarize their insights and thoughts,

repeating them to them for confirmation to ensure understanding. (Restatement). Deepen connections and turn dialogue into a rich tapestry of shared experiences and understanding.

Switch roles; now it's your partner's turn to lead the exchange. The conversation ends after both participants have completed their EDR response.

47.   **From Plain to Pain** - The cardholder will start by thinking of a negative adjective, such as "boring." The person next to them will then transform it, making it more negative and gloomy. For example, "boring" could become "mind-numbingly monotonous and soul-draining." The pattern continues, and the person who transformed the word will now say a regular word that the person next to them will transform. Feel free to incorporate current events, pop culture, social media, etc.

Continue the cycle until everyone has taken three turns. It's not just a game; it's a simple way to get creative, laugh, and connect through inventive expressions.

48. **Finding Humor in the Negative** - Share a recent negative or challenging experience, whether it's a frustrating situation, a mishap, or an annoyance. Describe the details of this experience.

Each group member needs to find something humorous or absurd in the negative experience shared by the cardholder. Try to identify a funny element, a quirky aspect, or an unexpected twist in the story that can bring laughter to the situation.

The game ends when everyone has contributed their humorous statements, including the storyteller, finding the lighter side of each negative experience shared.

49. **Laughing at Ourselves** - Start with a sarcastic, positive, affirming statement about yourself, then reveal a self-deprecating twist. Focus on a situation or trait of yourself that you find amusing. Embrace your quirks, but also bring laughter to the atmosphere.

For example,

Positively Sarcastic Statement: I'm a natural-born chef.

Self-Deprecating Twist: I attempted to cook a gourmet meal for myself, but the only thing I managed to master was burning water.

Continue sharing your self-deprecating jokes until everyone has contributed. Once each participant has shared their humorous tale, the laughter-filled exchange concludes.

50. **Comic Hero Carnival** - Create your self-deprecating superhero persona. Introduce yourself with a funny name and a unique superpower; for example, "I am Clumsy Crusader, and my superpower is the ability to trip over my cape, leaving villains in stitches."

Share your creative alter ego with the group, setting the stage for hilarity. Do this until everyone has introduced their unlikely superhero names and superpowers.

51. **From Common to Witty** - The cardholder will start by thinking of a positive adjective, such as "good." The person next to them will then transform it, elevating it to something witty and unique. For example, "good" could become "Oscar-worthy" or "Super awesome!" The pattern continues, and the person who transformed the word will now say a positive adjective that the person next to them will elevate. Feel free to incorporate current events, pop culture, social media, etc.

Keep the chain going until everyone has had three turns, and see how far you can take the descriptions, making each one more clever and unexpected than the last.

52. **2 Funny Truths, 1 Funny Lie Game** - Each player will take turns sharing three statements about themselves. Among these statements, two should be hilarious but true, while one should be equally funny but completely fabricated. After someone shares, the other players will guess which statement is the lie.

The game continues until everyone in the group has shared their three statements, creating an atmosphere of laughter and amusing revelations!

www.ingramcontent.com/pod-product-compliance
Lightning Source LLC
Chambersburg PA
CBHW060605080526
44585CB00013B/692